THE

SECRET POWER

OF

COVENANT

DESTINY IMAGE BOOKS BY KERRY KIRKWOOD

THE
SECRET POWER
OF
COVENANT

Unleashing God's
Protection, Power, and Prosperity
in Your Life

KERRY KIRKWOOD

DESTINY IMAGE® PUBLISHERS, INC.

P.O. Box 310, Shippensburg, PA 17257-0310

"Promoting Inspired Lives."

This book and all other Destiny Image, Revival Press, MercyPlace, Fresh Bread, Destiny Image Fiction, and Treasure House books are available at Christian bookstores and distributors worldwide.

For a U.S. bookstore nearest you, call 1-800-722-6774.

For more information on foreign distributors, call 717-532-3040.

Reach us on the Internet: www.destinyimage.com.

ISBN 13 TP: 978-0-7684-4247-2

ISBN 13 Ebook: 978-0-7684-8458-8

For Worldwide Distribution, Printed in thse U.S.A.

1 2 3 4 5 6 7 8 / 17 16 15 14 13

EVERYTHING GOD DOES

HE DOES IN

AND THROUGH COVENANT.

CONTENTS

INTRODUCTION

*It is the glory of God to conceal a matter, but the glory
of kings is to search out a matter* (PROVERBS 25:2).

I STARTED ON A mission to attempt to discover why some prayers
are answered and others are delayed and sometimes never actual-
ized. At least that was the starting point; somewhere in the course
of the search I had an Ah-Ha moment. It was right before me in
plain sight; it was so simple, yet I was looking for something heav-
ily theological. Here it is, and you may have already known this:
*God does nothing outside of covenant—everything He does is because of
covenant.* I have not been able to find any exception to this truth.
When I thought I had found an anomaly, I soon realized it was
connected in some way to a covenant in some form.

This is not a treatise on the seven major covenants of the Bible
from Adam to Abraham and on to Christ. There are plenty of books
that detail those from a theological position. This book is written as
a practical application of placing yourself in a position to get answers

THE SECRET POWER OF COVENANT

that affect every part of your life. I hope you will find answers to issues that have plagued your family and marriage for some time. In this book, you will discover how to search for promises that belong to you personally and have yet to be fulfilled. While reading these pages, I believe you will find personal applications you can use to make adjustments to areas that have hindered you from entering into the favor you so desired. This book was designed as a how-to book and provides important life-changing information. It's not the truth we hear or read that makes us free but the truth that we apply. But only when God's truth is applied will you be free.

Proverbs 13:12 says, *"Hope deferred makes the heart sick, but desire fulfilled is a tree of life."* Covenant is the capacity that allows us to claim particular promises of the Word of God. Where there are broken or fragmented covenants, those promises are deferred. We are in a time in our nation when broken covenants in marriage and in government have brought about deferred economic growth as well as deferred spiritual revelation and revival.

You will read stories of those who have discovered the secret power of covenant and the faith they used to enter into a powerful agreement with God. The impetus for writing this book was to see marriages strengthened and help those contemplating breaking sacred bonds to consider the unintended consequences that result from such selfish actions. For those who have been part of broken covenants, there is plenty of meat in these pages to lead them to healing and in some cases restoration. This book will also reveal areas where there has been resistance to breakthrough.

God so loved us He gave us a covenant that is so powerful it crushes the head of the serpent. Just think when we function under the canopy of covenant how blessed and favored our lives can be. Because God is a God of covenant, there is no way for us to please Him without being covenant keepers. Any time Israel stepped outside the boundaries of covenant and worshiped pagan idols, their enemies prevailed. Covenant is a boundary not for the purpose of confinement but for the purpose of liberty and protection from the attacks and predators of our souls.

———◆———

In 1977 I was starting out as a young under-experienced pastor ready to enter a world and culture that I knew nothing about. After only one month being at the tiny church in West Texas, I was confronted with every problem imaginable in a church. It would have been a tough road for any pastor, but especially for one who had no grid for the perversion and apathy I faced. The hardest part to understand was why the people who had been there for fourteen years did not object to what was obviously going on. They had become so used to hearing about the (former) pastor's fornication with various women in the church that it eventually became acceptable.

When I confronted the former pastor, he said to me, "Young man, when you get to my level of spirituality, God gives you the desires of your heart." He then quoted from First John saying if your heart condemns you not, then you have peace with God. He concluded saying, "I have peace with God." My world up to then had been sheltered from this type of attitude.

When I talked to some of the church leaders about confronting this sin, I was told we needed to forgive and leave it in the hands of the Holy Spirit.

I went to the church the following Wednesday morning and lay on the floor of the sanctuary and cried out to God. My prayer went something like this: "Father, I am sorry that I thought I could do this. These people don't like me. So if You could get me out of here and let me go back to my former quiet life, I will never ask to preach again. Amen." I was shocked by the response I received from the Lord. He said to me, "Do you remember when you prayed Philippians 3:10—that you wanted to know Me and the power of My resurrection and the fellowship of My suffering?" I did remember praying that, and then He said, "I brought you here to fellowship. If we are going to fellowship, then you need to know how I feel about this place. It grieves My heart as well."

I never really thought about God being grieved over something, but He does grieve. I received instructions from Him as to what I was to do, and eventually the matter was cleansed out, and I was able to place a godly person in that position. I discovered firsthand what happens to a church that moves out of covenant with God and becomes so calloused that truth is cast aside solely for the sake of tradition.

God is serious about covenant and about His word. Where there is breaking of covenant, there is the loss of proceeding revelation from the Holy Spirit and dullness of hearing the word of the Lord.

You will also find in these pages the joy people experience when they walk with God in covenant and the prosperity that follows.

May your eyes be enlightened so you may know the hope of His calling and the richness of His inheritance for you. May the Lord bless your life with favor as you read this book!

1

DISCOVERING COVENANT

—————◆—————

I T WAS WINTERTIME and it had been a long, difficult night because my wife and I had been up with our six-month-old daughter who was very ill. For several days we did the best we could, but her cold turned into serious congestion and an ear infection. We called our pediatrician and were told to bring Kristen in immediately.

In the examination room, the doctor examined her carefully. Kristen was so miserable that she couldn't stop crying. As a young parent of a suffering baby, the helpless feeling I had was almost too much to bear; I so wished I could take the pain for her. Her cries got louder when the doctor checked her ears. The pediatrician told us that she had an acute infection and needed to have tubes surgically placed in her ears for the infection to subside and the fluid to drain. Without the tubes she would be prone to more infections and possible hearing loss. I was stunned. *Where would I get the money for the procedure?* We would do anything for our children, so we knew we had to go through with the surgery. The surgery was set for the next morning.

As we drove home, I thought about all the recent events in our lives since we had agreed to take on church planting. It had been a year since my first church attempt in West Texas. We now were going to plant a church in East Texas. We had recently moved to Tyler from Amarillo in response to an invitation to start the church. It was a very hard decision to leave Amarillo and our families, friends, and the terrific support system that we had grown up in. We both wished we lived closer to our folks, especially now with a new baby. We felt so alone.

I thought I knew that the Lord had directed us to East Texas, but now I was beginning to have some doubts. I had told the Lord that I would give five years of my life to being in Tyler. We had moved our young family to what seemed a world away—away from all that we had grown up with, and all we had known and loved. Our secure little world was now being shaken.

When we returned home from the doctor's office, I took Kristen to her room to give her the prescription and a bottle of milk. As she lay there laboring to breathe due to the heavy congestion, I started to blame myself for deciding to bring our family to this place that seemed at the moment God-forsaken. I then recalled a special encounter I had with the Lord over coming to Tyler. I had said to Him, "If this is right for me to go, then why does it feel so wrong?" I'm sure I sounded like I was singing a whiney Country and Western song. Then God said to me so sweetly, "If you will go and represent Me to the people, I will take care of every need that will come up and your children will lack for nothing, and I will be your healer." I realized that God was giving grounds for covenant. This encounter had taken place almost a year before our need, and I had almost forgotten what had been promised.

I went back into Kristen's room, and overlooking her bed I said, "God, You told me that You would take care of this need we have with our baby, and I believe You sent me here. So if You don't heal her, then I will take that as permission to pack up and leave 'cause I don't want to be where I don't have You with me."

In my mind I pondered, *God, if You are not here with us (and Your presence?), then do I have the right to leave and go back to Amarillo?* Then I heard the Lord say, "You have the right to claim your promises and healing over your daughter." That word of covenant from the Lord immediately clicked in my spirit, and I felt a shift of strength.

When we arrived at the hospital for the scheduled surgery, I handed Kristen to the nurse. With one last kiss on her forehead, she was taken to be prepared for surgery. We settled in for the waiting period knowing I had placed her in the arms of our Covenantal Father, believing what He had said to me almost a year earlier.

To our surprise, thirty minutes later, the nurse who had taken Kristen into surgery returned with her. I will never forget her words to us, "This is not the same baby we saw yesterday. The doctor looked into her ears just now and could not find any fluid or infection." She said, "We don't know what happened, but take her home, she's fine." After a quick testimony to the nurse, we left weeping and thanking God for the miracle. I had discovered that God wanted me to remind Him of His promise to us. It wasn't that God has a short memory, but it was me who needed to remember that God lives inside of His own Word; and if I was to delight in what He had for me, I had to learn to live inside those same boundaries.

COVENANT—FOUNDATIONAL PRINCIPLE

This is the first time I remember tapping into the power of covenant. It wasn't until years later that I began to grasp and walk in an understanding of covenant. The more I learn about the Father, the more I understand about covenant. The more I understand about covenant, the more my appreciation grows for Jesus' sacrifice. The more I appreciate His sacrifice, the stronger and more effective my prayers are. The more I see the results of prayer and His prophetic word, the more I pursue Him to find out more of His ways.

Covenant is a foundational principle of our faith. Covenant is a foundation that we build upon. But it is also a place and a position. Covenant allows us to accept our position as co-heirs with Christ and be seated in covenant with Christ Jesus (see Ephesians 1 and 2). When we understand covenant, we will pray differently with a targeted focus for answers.

With something this important it is a wonder why more people aren't walking in this truth and power. An independent spirit causes us to lose sight of the power that is inside of covenant and make choices based upon what feels good at the moment without realizing that they may be violating covenant.

COVENANT DEFINED

Covenant is a well-known term in a business environment. We use the term so often. In spite of being familiar, the definition has shifted. It literally means a contract between two parties which are of equal ability to perform the agreement. In the business world a covenant is used in contracts to define agreements that contain a penalty if they are broken. We depend on covenants to buy a house, get paid, get married, and buy a cell phone. Without covenants our culture would grind to a halt because business and commerce are built on a platform of agreements. Covenants spell out the responsibilities and liabilities of the parties involved. In business contracts each party tries to get the most benefits with the least amount of liability.

When we think of a covenant in the Old Testament, the first response is usually Noah and the rainbow. In biblical terms, a covenant refers to an agreement between God and His people. God made covenants with Noah, Abraham, Moses, and David. Each of these covenants was like rungs in a ladder moving upward. Each covenant represented a new promise from God to man. In the New Testament, God gave Jesus as the fulfillment of the New Covenant. Let's take the familiar verse of John 3:16: *"For God so loved the world, that He gave* [a covenant] *His only begotten Son, that whoever believes in Him* [the covenant] *shall not perish, but have eternal life"* [by the covenant, which is the gift of God]. When we receive Jesus as Savior, we are receiving the covenant of God both into our hearts and blessing of God's covenant over our lives. Everything God does He does because of covenant. I have not found any place where God responded in power or performed miracles without covenant being involved. If this is true, then how much more do we need to understand the secret power of covenant and how it affects every part of our lives?

COVENANTS AND CONTRACT DIFFERENCES

Many marriages today begin with a contractual mindset instead of a covenantal heart. In contracts each party defines the limits of his or her liabilities and divides the responsibilities. Jesus did not make a contract with us—He made a covenant. He did not limit the liabilities; in fact, He took upon Himself all the liabilities of sin and gave us total freedom from liabilities or penalties of sin. He took upon Himself all the responsibilities for us and paid the price—and we received all the benefits.

In some marriages one or both spouses manipulate one another to gain less liability and more benefits. When a true biblical covenant is in place, a husband will take on the model that Jesus gave us for the church. As a husband, I am to take on all liabilities without any demand for benefits because of the love factor. Love without a heart of covenant can be quickly lost when circumstances go awry. When covenant is practiced, it takes you through the rough spots. Ask the Holy Spirit to birth a spirit of covenant in your marriage. Jesus laid down His life because of the covenant He had with His Father.

One of the reasons I wanted to write about covenant is to clear up some bad theology that has distorted and twisted the true meaning of covenant. It is not about demanding our rights as believers. The only rights we have are due to His taking on all the liabilities and the penalty for sin. We can ask in faith believing and He wants to answer not because of our theology or how much we understand about faith. He answers us because He is in covenant with His Father. Jesus said in John 14:14, *"If you ask Me anything in My name, I will do it."* It was all about revealing the goodness of His Father.

Perhaps one reason why some find it difficult to live in covenant is because they have never experienced the love of the Father or even an earthly father. Contracts are very sterile and surface, but covenants are intimate and based upon one who is the stronger standing in behalf of the weaker. Jesus took our place not based upon a contract but on covenant sworn and backed by His own blood.

REDEFINING COVENANT BY THE HOLY SPIRIT

For the Body of Christ, I firmly believe that this is a time that the Father wants us to have a new and different understanding of covenant. We need to deconstruct our expectations and definitions of covenant and discover the true meaning of what covenant is if we want to walk in the spiritual power, giftings, experience the power of Christ's resurrection, and open doors for revival, but most of all be witnesses of His light and carriers of the signs, wonders, and miracles of God.

When we understand covenant more deeply, then it will expand and change the mindsets and beliefs that have defined God to us and break through some religious traditions. Once the Holy Spirit has defined more clearly who He is, then we will become refined in who He is, not what He is. When the Holy Spirit defines who He is inside of us, then our spirit-self becomes refined into more of the image of God. In short, some people prefer a make-do lifestyle, whereas the Holy Spirit prefers a make-over lifestyle.

The more my understanding of God's covenant blessing grew, the more my love for God and others grew. I could finally cast off the orphan spirit and mindsets that negatively affected my relationships. I noticed after teaching this at my church and other places where I ministered; I could not help but notice a more dynamic worship and deepening relationships among the people. Embracing covenant, I was able to prophesy with greater strength and specificity. When I learned to integrate covenantal Word thought and meditation of what God promises through His covenant into my life, striving to "become" ceased. As we continued to walk out covenant with each other at Trinity Fellowship, we saw a greater amount of the power of God released around and through us. We saw God expanding our boundaries personally, spiritually, and financially—for the glory of His Kingdom.

GOD DOES ALL THINGS THROUGH COVENANT

Everything God does He does through covenant. Covenant is God's operating system; it is His economy. One of the incorrect perceptions about the nature of our culture is that everything begins with us and is about us. This is totally opposite of covenant thinking. The idea of covenant begins in Heaven, proceeds from the throne room of God, and flows down to us for the sole purpose of revealing the love and compassion God has for all humankind. Sadly, there are people who approach salvation on a contract basis and not in covenant. When they find the benefits are wonderful and do not allow covenant to take hold of their hearts, they forget that Jesus said in John 14:15, *"If you love Me, you will keep* [obey] *My commandments."*

The boundaries are there not for restriction but for protection. If the benefits are poured out outside of covenant, then we approach the relationship not with love but with the idea *I married Jesus for His money.* Soon after the ceremony, in contract marriages, the one who is outside of covenant will drift away after other lovers who steal and eventually will destroy them. Covenant is not about us forcing God's hand to do what we want. Instead, true covenant flows from God to us. We need to be aligned to God's covenant instead of using covenant to make God align to our wishes. Being conformed to the image of Christ has a lot to do with being conformed to His will—and His will is His covenant. God's will doesn't exist outside of the canopy of His covenant.

LET US MAKE MAN

One of the first examples of the power of covenant is in creation. When there was covenant then there was creation. In Genesis 1:26, *"Then God said, 'Let Us make man in Our image, according to Our likeness,"* God agreed with Himself, the Trinity, and man was created.

Man was imagined in the mind of God and then as the Father, Son, and Holy Spirit agreed, man was made. In the Gospel of John, it says:

> *In the beginning was the Word, and the Word was with God, and the Word was God. He was with God in the beginning. Through him all things were made; without*

him nothing was [created] *made that has been made* (John 1:1-3 NIV).

When there is covenant and the word is spoken and declared, then it has the ability to cause things to come into being and be created. When we tap into the mind of God and are aware of what His will is, then we can pray and declare and it will be on earth as it is in Heaven. The very image of God is on the inside of us, and God stamped it there by saying it to be so. The potential of living in covenant is already in our spirit. The soul or mind is where we have the problem reconciling what we are going through with what God said. Covenant has the last word; it is the final judgment. At times I react because I don't have vision to see the end of something.

Covenantal vision sees the end from the beginning and keeps us in perfect peace because we know the result is going to be covered by His will.

THE SEED OF COVENANT

I remember as a young boy planting gardens with my dad in Northwest Texas. We would go to Wilborns, a plant nursery business. This particular nursery was known for the high quality of seeds, especially vegetable seeds. In those days, many of the seeds were loose and hand-selected rather than prepackaged. I said to Dad as he held a handful of corn seed, "Doesn't look like much corn." He answered, "They will become much more than I have in my hand if we plant them correctly."

Genesis 1:11 reveals a picture of creation multiplied. Though God created everything originally with the spoken word, the miracle of multiplication takes over from the original design. The life is in the seed. God created seed to reproduce, and the potential that is in the tiny seed is seen only through imagination. If seeds are altered, as seeds have been today, they are called hybrid seeds.

A hybrid is defined as a mixture of two different species of something to form one new thing. A hybrid seed cannot produce more seed for the next generation or season of planting. It may produce a crop, but the seeds inside the fruit are sterile and don't have life in them. One generation may prosper and the next generation fails. Why is it?

When we alter and try to improve on what God said, it won't prosper. In the Old Testament you can find where one king is successful and then the next king fails and causes Israel to go into judgment because of idolatry. The second king failed to realize that the prosperity handed to him from the former favored king came through the covenant God had made with Israel. The second king became self-promoting and arrogant and made decisions outside of the boundaries of covenant. We do the same thing when we start altering God's original creation, *"And God said...and it was so."* For instance, let there be light. During times of prosperity we forget what brought us to the point of blessing and we start making hybrid seeds, disregarding God's covenant that provides multiplication of all good things in life.

Discover and covet the promises that have been spoken over your family—don't let a hybrid word creep into the generations to follow so that your legacy is lost in the first generation after you are gone. If there has been a chronic problem in health, marriages, and finances, consider repenting and revisiting what your covenant boundaries should have been.

In paradise God told Adam that he could eat from any fruit tree, and I believe that included the Tree of Life. The only boundary to this wonderful relationship concerned the forbidden Tree of the Knowledge of Good and Evil. *Eden* means the Place of His Presence and the Place of His Pleasure. Wow, what glory there must have been on a daily basis. Fear had not been introduced; there was no division in the relationship between Adam and his wife, Eve.

Everything was perfect until the day the woman ventured outside of God's orders. She was creating a hybrid seed. The serpent rationalized that God didn't really mean she would die. In fact, she would be more like God, thus creating the hybrid of an independent spirit.

The hybrid here was to mix the glory of God with the knowledge of good and evil. The devil knew the only way the canopy of glory would lift was for the covenant to be breached. When they ate of the forbidden fruit, the glory departed and they were uncovered like orphans. They had said no to their Father and cast off their covering. Their hybrid covenant now cost them, and all those to follow, hard labor to grow things and pained childbirth.

If we really understood the power of covenant, we would be more cautious when rationalizing our decisions.

First Peter 1:23 says we have not been born again with perishable (corruptible, hybrid) seed but the imperishable (incorruptible) seed which is the Word of God. The glory of being in aligned relationship to God ensures we will reproduce after His kind and His Word. For example, one reason we don't see prayer answered is because we are not praying with incorruptible seed. Much of our prayer is simply trying to convince God of our neediness. Instead we are to pray using incorruptible seed that when planted in faith will grow beyond what we thought was even possible. The life of the seed comes from being under covenant.

HOPE IS FREE FROM SHAME

There is something about the human nature that loves to hope and hope for the future. We are called to have hope, faith, and love. But in life we are motivated to step from a place of hope and into a place of faith and from there move into obedience. Obedience is a sign that we really believe His covenant is true. For instance, do you know that tithing is a test to see how closely we believe God. Some think that tithing was only an Old Testament concept. The word tithe means a "tenth"; ten is the number of testing like the Ten Commandments. There were ten lepers who were healed, and only one came back to give thanks. There were ten plagues used to test Pharaoh to let the Hebrews leave slavery.

The tithe was a test to see if the people would honor God with the first of their prosperity. When they gave the tithe, the promises of God were lived out. The tithe is seen also as seed. When we withhold the seed that belongs to God we are stating that we don't fully believe the covenant. The seed of God's Word gives us hope. As we embrace that hope it grows and expands until the hope catapults us into higher and higher levels of faith, which in turn expand our love and relationship with the Father.

THE *NOW* OF GOD

If we would press into the *now of God* today instead of pushing hope into the far future, we would see signs and wonders. Have you ever heard someone say, "One of these days I will be healed," or "One of these days I will have my miracle"? It's easier to place into the future what we desire than to press in at the moment. The Bible says, *Now faith is* and *Today is the day of salvation*. We will do most anything to avoid pressure and yet pressure can be a catalyst for salvation. In Matthew 9:20 a woman had been suffering for twelve years from hemorrhaging. She pressed through the crowd and said within herself, *If I can just touch the hem of His garment I will be healed*. She didn't think about another day or another perhaps. She moved past her fears of disappointment and held assurance in the highest part of her mind—she broke through all of the taboo of traditions.

We are not called to be passive believers who live in the hope of a better day. We are called to press past the unbelief to receive. Living under a covenant of faith inspires us to break through into the now. By pushing God into the future, it gives us an excuse to be complacent. We love to be comfortable with where we are. We are the greatest procrastinators, more than any other species on the planet. When we declare that God is *now*, it changes things. Revival is at the very moment when we believe God is in the *now*.

As I explained in my book *The Power of Imagination*, God wants us to use our creative imagination to see God at work at the present. Here are some thoughts to ponder:

- Do you imagine God *now* or someday?

- What do you imagine about God and do you imagine Him working today?

- Do you see in your imagination the healing and miracles and salvations?

- Can you imagine creative miracles taking place today? Why not today?

- Do you believe that there is a divine connection between you and God *now?*

- With God right now, can you sense Him inside or around you?

Scriptures say many times and even Jesus cried out to the crowds, "If you have ears to hear, then listen up" (see Mark 4:9 and others).

BE IN THE AMEN

One of the ways we can experience God in the *now* is to be in the AMEN. Amen means, "now so be it". Amen is agreeing with the prompting of His Word—spoken in the present tense—*right now*.

In Genesis, the Trinity of God came together in agreement. They said, let us together make man. Blessing of unity, imagined in the mind of God, and then covenant resulted in the creation of man. Man was created from their agreement and words. Just consider the favor you would incur if the agreement of your words were synchronized with His. Under the canopy of His covenant no evil shall befall you there. Under the shadow of His covenant fear can't come at you from behind. Under His covering you have the right and power to deny access to sickness. You have the authority to say to your enemy, "Flee! You are trespassing on holy ground because it is ground that His covenant is covering."

REVIVAL HAPPENS WHEN?

Revival is at the very moment when we receive God for who He is. Revival does not happen when He is going to do it in the future. It is often easier to talk about the God of the Old Testament versus the God of Right Now. One example of this is the man who was asked if he wanted to buy a life insurance policy and he replied, "No, because I'm not thinking of dying for at least twenty more years."

Revival is not someone who comes to the church with a suit-case of sermons. Revival is not based on a calendar or schedule or tent. Revival is in us. So it means that any point in time when you allow God to arise and break through, revival happens (but it works better collectively). It happens when you say to people, "Can you see that God is the one who healed me?" Revival is in you... and God happening in and through you.

LET GOD ARISE—REVELATION OF HIM IN THE MOMENT

When we see and embrace that He is the God who heals me now, then the power of God can move more freely through your life so that you are a conduit for revival. Whatever God is to you right now is the level of revival that you will have.

As Jesus appeared, so we become like Him (see 1 John 3). This passage of Scripture is not just referring to future tense. It also reveals that how He appears right now can bring a right now change.

The word revival is translated as resuscitate me. We ask the Spirit of God to breathe into us the Breath of God. When we experience the covenant, we see the heart of the loving Father. The more we embrace His covenant, the more prosperous His seed can become.

Discussed in the next chapter are the characteristics of covenant and how those principles impact your life.

Lord Jesus,

I pray over those reading these pages—may they absorb the true meaning of being married to You through the covenant You made with Your Father. You knew that we could not keep the covenant, so You took our place and made covenant in behalf of us. I pray over marriages that are struggling and businesses that are just barely surviving, and I ask for supernatural intervention; reveal Yourself as the Lord God who keeps covenant and mercy.

Amen!

2

PROMISES OF COVENANT

———◆———

THE POLIO EPIDEMIC was in full swing in 1948 when my oldest sister, Vonna, came down with polio on her fourth birthday. My mother had only been born again a few short weeks when on July 15, 1948, Mom had given Vonna a birthday party with about fifteen of her friends attending. But Vonna was sick with severe dizziness, ringing in her ears, and neck pain. The small town doctor came to the house and examined her but he really didn't know what was wrong. He thought it might be the flu.

The next morning Mom couldn't wake Vonna and realized something was terribly wrong. The doctor was summoned again. This time he was very alarmed. "I believe she has polio," he said. My parents rushed her to the nearest hospital, Saint Anthony's in Amarillo, Texas. She was immediately put into quarantine until tests confirmed or disproved the diagnosis.

Three doctors confirmed that Vonna had Bulbar Polio as well as Spinal Meningitis. Her left side was paralyzed and she was in a deep coma running a 105-degree temperature most of the time for nine days. Her throat was paralyzed, so water had to be dropped onto her tongue to keep it from cracking open. On the ninth day the doctor told my mother that Vonna probably wouldn't live through the night. And if by some miracle she did live, he said Vonna would be severely mentally disabled as well as physically crippled.

My mother, living out her young faith, was steadfast that the God she had come to know would step into the picture at any moment. Although she didn't know what to call the confidence that she had for the miracle, she knew she had a promise from God that her children would be protected from the evil one. She placed Vonna into the care of the Lord knowing that she had done all that was required from her, which was to believe with all her heart—not in the doctors' report, but the report of the Lord (see Isa. 53:1).

The small town of Stratford had turned out to pray for Vonna at one of the local churches because it terrorized the whole town that polio had hit our community. On the tenth morning, my dad went to the hospital to see how she was doing. It was then Vonna came out of the coma for the first time in ten days. She spoke to Dad, telling him he had a smudge on his face.

There was such rejoicing at what God had done! The doctors were totally amazed that there was no residual affect from this dreaded disease. After further examination she was released from the hospital the next day. Her healing was a testimony to the whole town of Stratford, Texas. Vonna is now 68 years old and goes into the jails and prisons telling her story of God's healing power.

Mother learned the power of covenant firsthand. She continued to instill this principle to all of her children. When we had something difficult in front of us, she would ask, "What promise are you connecting with this issue?" She would quickly remind us of Second Corinthians 1:20 that says, *"As many as are the promises of God, in Him they are yes; therefore also through Him is our Amen to the glory of God through us."* After she would quote the verse, she would again ask, "Do you have a Yes in your heart for what you are believing for? Are you in complete agreement with God's Word? If so, then you must have an Amen, which means 'Let it be done.'"

The promises of God are based and centered on His covenant to you. A promise without something to back it up is simply wishful thinking. If Jesus had promised us we could have authority over the devil and not backed it with His resurrection from the dead, it would only have been a nice, well-thought-out sermon. Because He conquered death, which the devil ruled over, we now have the promise because it was backed up through His blood covenant.

As you read these pages, are you facing something that is overwhelming to you? Allow the Holy Spirit to give you the promise you need to stand on to overcome it. Once you have the promise (ammunition), let the Yes of the Lord sound off inside your spirit so that you will know that things are going to turn around. You may be asking, "How do I know when I have that promised word?" The Scripture that comes alive inside of you will back a covenant promise, and you know that you know you are on firm ground. Belief will begin, but your faith takes over until you see the reality of your promise.

In Matthew 18:19 Jesus said that, "if two of you agree on earth about anything that they may ask, it shall be done for them by My Father who is in Heaven."

The word agreed that Jesus used *(homologeo)* means to say the same thing; the word touching *(peri)* means to go through or to pierce. Jesus is teaching us to get on the same page with His Word and say the same thing with our words, and when we do, we will pierce or break through the obstacle. We should understand by saying the same thing as His word says is not just an exercise in repeating some spiritual mantra; on the contrary, we are saying Yes to the promise that is backed up through His covenant. If only mere words written and not acted upon through the sacrifice of

God's Son, then we could conclude there is no power. In reality, the Yes and Amen pierce the gates of hell and release what has been held captive through sin and disobedience.

COVENANT PURPOSE

As discussed in the last chapter, God does everything through covenant. This is easy to understand because we know that the Word of the Lord is true and the Word of God is His covenant.

There are several advantages and purposes of covenants. In the broadest sense, a covenant is like an improved contract between humankind and God. A contract's purpose is to limit our liabilities and to protect our rights. A covenant with God takes on all liabilities and we give up our rights unconditionally.

The first covenant mentioned in Scripture is marriage. Covenant (Hebrew-*bereeth*) means to cut. The term actually meant "cutting of covenant." In Genesis 2:21, Adam was formed out of the dust of the earth and woman came out of Adam by the cutting or opening up his side. There was cutting involved when covenant was made between Adam and Eve. It is important to note that the woman was not formed from the dust like Adam. God brought her out of man, thus the name wo-man, or out of man. This is why Adam exclaimed that she *"is now bone of my bones, and flesh of my flesh"* (Gen. 2:23). Covenant comes out of our hearts not some wedding contract that is written on paper. The passage goes on to say, *"For this reason a man shall leave his father and his mother and be joined to his wife"* (Gen. 2:24). The covenant was part of each of them. God was prophetically saying man will want to leave his father and mother; He said this when there had never before been a father or mother. The purpose that covenant draws out becomes our destiny. Covenant is not just a word made up out of thin air, it comes out of something and takes form into something in our destiny.

When Christ was on the cross and the solider took the spear and pierced Him, blood and water flowed out (see John 19:34). Again covenant was being cut between Christ and His Bride. Just as Eve was taken from the side of the first Adam, so the Second Adam, Jesus, had a bride taken from His side. The blood that flowed from His side was the purchase price to redeem His Bride. The sacrifice is always greater than the judgment.

Covenant makes two become one so there are no longer two identities. Romans 8:1 states, *"There is now no condemnation for those who are in Christ Jesus"* [covenant]. When we take on His identity and cast away our identity of sin, we are not common law believers, where He might leave us for another—we are married to Jesus. He told us that He would never leave or forsake us. So He says over you right now, "You are bone of My bone and flesh of My flesh, you can now be joined to Me and live." Now we gladly give up our rights and take what He promised. Without the revelation of God's gracious covenant, we keep falling back under the control of sin. Covenant cuts us off from our past and connects us to our destiny.

The idea of covenant was originated by God for the purpose of identifying those who are His. Throughout the Old Testament covenants were identified by acts of obedience that could be seen outwardly. The New Covenant was enacted through the obedience of Jesus who laid down His life so we could have life more abundantly (see John 10:10).

SIGNS OF COVENANT

We are recipients of the covenant of Abraham. Now, every covenant has a sign to confirm that it's a covenant. Noah witnessed a sign; what was it? The rainbow; a sign of His covenant that He would not destroy the earth again with a flood (see Gen. 8:21).

Every time you see a rainbow, you're looking at a covenantal sign. He has a covenant with creation, that He will not destroy creation.

The covenant God made with Abraham in Genesis 17 is significant. He is saying, here is the sign of the covenant that I have with Abraham—circumcision. God says you will circumcise the foreskin of every male, and this circumcision is a sign that you have been obedient to My covenant. It is a covenantal sign. Israel, the Hebrews, were the only people throughout that region who ever practiced circumcision. So God was giving this as a sign of His covenant to separate His chosen people through the cutting away of the flesh—separating them from all of the pagan nations. Idolatry and human sacrificing were prevalent among the nations that surrounded Israel. The males would lead the families from generation to generations. If the leaders of families were not separated from the barbaric practices of the land, mixture would infiltrate the people and lead them away from the only true and living God.

I hope to show you how covenants mark our spiritual inheritance and destinies. Covenant is not just a theological concept, it's the reality that separates the fallen nature of humankind that continues to grow more perverse every generation from God's intended blessing for those who carry His covenant.

Proverbs 22:28 (Deut. 27:17) says, *"Do not move the ancient boundary* [landmarks] *which your fathers have set."* Other passages show that a curse comes for moving the boundary lines. Though these verses refer to marking the ownership of property, we are able to extract a spiritual principle relevant for us today. The reason for the boundary was to show separation between ownerships. Ownership gives legal rights for certain things to take place on that land. The authority belongs to the one holding the deed to the property. Some people wonder why circumstances seem to go against them and they are constantly battling the devil over even the simplest of things. Well here is one of the biggest and yet hidden reasons:

Nevertheless, the firm foundation of God stands, having this seal, "The Lord knows those who are His," and, "Everyone who names the name of the Lord is to abstain from wickedness" (2 Timothy 2:19).

The foundation is strong as long as it is on the right property. If we are living life from the ownership of Christ, He knows us. The sign that we are accepting His covenant or boundary is through departing from iniquity—abstaining from wickedness, which means lawlessness. The landmark of this covenant is in the heart. Lawless behavior is not taking into account the landmarks that He has written upon our hearts (see 2 Cor. 3:3); and when those boundaries are moved or compromised, the gates are open for evil trespassers into our lives.

In the New Testament Paul describes it like this, *"In Him* [Christ] *you were also circumcised with a circumcision made without hands, in the removal of the body of the flesh by the circumcision of Christ"* (Col. 2:11). This circumcision of the heart sets a boundary between the kingdom of darkness and the Kingdom of God. It is a line that the devil is not permitted to cross and we are not permitted to move or alter or adjust to fit our cultural changes. The Bible says that Jesus Christ is the same yesterday and forever (see Heb. 13:8). This statement also means that He has not changed the landmarks that keep us in covenantal protection. The territory you frequent is the authority you give to rule your life.

SIGN OF DELIVERANCE

God is so serious about covenant that He won't alter His Word no matter who it is. Let me give an example. Exodus 4:24 is the account of Moses being sent back to Egypt to lead the Hebrews out of slavery after the burning bush experience. Verse 24 says it came about at the lodging place on the way that the Lord met

Moses and sought to put him to death. Zipporah, his wife, took took a flint and cut off the foreskin of her son and tossed at Moses' feet (see Exod. 4:24-26). This is a very interesting picture. Moses heads for Egypt under the orders of God to do a job, and on his way to fulfill this mission he encounters God who attempts to kill him. Obviously if God wanted to knock off Moses, that would not be a problem for Him. It did, however, get Moses' attention.

The issue came down to covenant. Moses was going to perform the miracles in front of Pharaoh in order to convince this pagan king to release God's people. Moses was attempting to go and do miracles without being in covenant because he had not obeyed God and circumcised his son. The authority Moses would carry was based upon his covenant relationship with God; and if he was not compliant with God's orders, then he would be powerless before Pharaoh and in rebellion to God. As important as Moses was to God's plans for His people, God would not circumvent His covenant.

Exodus 12 accounts the exodus of the Hebrews out of Egypt. The sign that would separate the Hebrews from the judgment that was to fall upon Egypt was the blood from a lamb. The blood was to be placed on the top and side posts of the door. Every person inside the house that was marked with the lamb's blood was protected. In verse 13 God promises the Hebrews, *"when I see the blood I will pass over you, and no plague will befall you to destroy you when I strike the land of Egypt."* Again the covenant God used marked the people of God and kept them from the wrath.

In First Samuel 16, God told Samuel when he was to anoint a new king, *"Man looks at the outward appearance, but the Lord looks at the heart."* Because we know that God was looking for the blood on the door of the Hebrews in Egypt, we can also be assured that He has placed a sign within us that He sees by looking upon our hearts.

I believe there is an unseen mark upon people's lives who have fully allowed the covenant of God to cover them. I also am convinced that the devil knows his bounds as well and knows that he can enter the house of a family that is uncovered. Though people may think they are rich and have need of nothing, the truth is they are wretched and marked by the enemy for destruction. Generational curses can be traced back to broken covenants that have given access to the evil one.

I am reminded of the son of a friend of mine. The young man grew up in a middle class family and enjoyed the benefits of a good Christian home. He began to press the boundaries of curfews and lie about his friends. The son started despising the protected family environment and wanted to be like others who had no restraints on them. He continued to enjoy all that his family offered even though he was thinking the grass would be greener elsewhere. The time came when the young man stretched his wings, so to speak, and left home. Communication between him and his family became less and less as the years flew by. He was not prospering, he wasn't sure from month to month where or with whom he would be living. In his own words, "I didn't have a dollar in my pocket." He survived off of other peoples' generosity.

My friend continued to pray over his son; he longed for his son to be restored to the values that he knew would protect his life. There were times when the young man was almost killed but the covering of his father kept a lifeline out. Then one day, just like the prodigal son in Luke 15, the young man came to the point of remembering that in his father's house there was plenty, *I always knew I had a place to go home to,* he thought. The difference in this story is that this son didn't go back to the home of his childhood—he went back to the covenant his father had between his family and God. He became successful and is enjoying covenant protection over his house today.

We can mark our children with the promise of God from Isaiah 54 that says our children shall be taught of the Lord and great peace shall be upon them. No weapon formed against them shall prosper and any voice raised against them shall be found to be false, for this is the heritage of the servants of the Lord.

PROSPERITY OF COVENANT

Galatians 3:13-14 says, "Christ redeemed us from the curse of the Law, having become a curse for us—for it is written, 'Cursed is everyone who hangs on a tree'—in order that the blessing of Abraham might come to the Gentiles, so that we would receive the promise of the Spirit through faith."

This truth connects the covenant that God gave to Abraham to the covenant we enjoy as believers today. Genesis 12:3 declares that God wanted to bless Abraham so that through him all the families of the earth would be blessed. In order for blessing to be passed on to others it has to begin somewhere. Abraham was the starting point for covenant blessing and prosperity to be passed down through the generations. Jesus became the connector to connect the blessing of Abraham to the promise of the Spirit through faith. The Old Covenant of blessing could not bring the promise of the Spirit. The promise of the Spirit according to John 14 would guide us into all truth and would convince and convict us of sin. With the covenant of the Spirit, I don't have to guess between good and evil. The Holy Spirit is the executor of the estate of Christ.

COVENANT CONFIRMS PROSPERITY

You shall remember the Lord your God, for it is He who is giving you the power to make wealth, that He may confirm His covenant which He swore to your fathers... (Deuteronomy 8:18).

It is important for us to know that wealth is not a sign of God's covenant. However for those who do have wealth, if they truly understand covenant they will confirm God's favor through giving. Through covenant God gives us the authority to make (not get) wealth. Prosperity will establish the fact it is God who gave me this wealth; but to say that those who are not wealthy are not in covenant is simply not true. Inside the dominion of covenant is favor. Depending on the stewardship and trust we are given, God decides whether more authority to handle wealth will be given.

NATURAL LAWS AND LAW OF COVENANT

God has set in place principles that can be followed. There are natural laws like there are spiritual laws. Gravity is a natural law that can be overcome by understanding the law of aerodynamics and thrust. But the law of gravity doesn't change. Gravity will always want to pull us back to earth no matter how long we have been in the air. Likewise, there are consumer products made to make life easier. In the instruction manual, the manufacturer specifies the use of the product and its limited use. When the product is used for something other than its design, then it is being used in violation of manufacturing specifications. For example, automobiles are designed to take us from one place to another, for the purpose of transportation. When a car is used to knock down a tree, the result can be fatal for the car and the driver.

Similarly, when we function inside the principles of covenant, the full potential of God's intentions are experienced. When those principles are violated, the result is not God's best or His will. Often there are those who get angry with God and blame Him for the results of their violations. Though He does not love us any less for violating and stepping out of covenant, the results due to breaching His covenant are laid at our door.

People send me emails asking why a prophetic word or promise of God they have received has not come to pass. One of the reasons for the lack of fulfillment could be the heart condition of the person. Remember that covenant is meant to change us to conform to God's will. We have to be willing to change and yield ourselves to God's plan. Remember circumcision in the New Testament is always about the heart. If the heart is not bending toward intimacy with the Lord and lining up with His plans, then chances are a person will experience a great measure of disappointment and waiting. If you aren't experiencing what you believe God has promised for you, then it might be a good time to ask the Spirit of Truth to align any areas that have become a mixture of light and darkness.

NEW COVENANT IS WRITTEN UPON THE HEART

Because God intends to extend His influence over our lives, He's saying, "Walk with Me, and see what I'll do. Test Me, and see if I'll not open the windows of Heaven." Where's the sign of the covenant written on the heart? The Lord declares it in Jeremiah 31:31-33 saying in a prophecy concerning the coming Messiah or Jesus:

> "...*I will make a new covenant* with the house of Israel and with the house of Judah, not like the covenant which I made with their fathers* [Moses] *in the day I took them by the hand to bring them out of the land of Egypt, My covenant which they broke, although I was a husband to them," declares the Lord. "But this is the covenant which I will make with the house of Israel after those days," declares the Lord, "I will put My law within them and on their heart...."*

This is not referring to the heart as a physical organ that pumps blood, but the spiritual heart within each of us. Our spiritual hearts say, "This is right, this is righteous, and this is the right thing to do." Not being moved by circumstantial external evidences, but living from within. Not letting the external issues dictate to all the things we do, but living for what is righteousness inside of us. God is saying, "I'm going to write it inside your heart; and when I write it inside your heart, then nothing is impossible if you believe."

If you are struggling with the cares of life and have not found any relief or favor, begin a change that will lead you to breaking out of an old pattern that has you locked inside. The only truth that makes us free is not the truth we hear but the truth we apply. The Holy Spirit may be speaking to you to break off unholy alliances with those who have soiled your garment of praise. Or you may be led to repent and ask the Lord to forgive you for not being a covenant giver because you are withholding forgiveness to others and withholding the tithe that belongs to God. Allow Him to reinstate the landmarks that will protect you—and bless you.

> *Dear Lord,*
>
> *Thank You for Your design and purpose of covenant. Thank You for the blessing of Your covenant and for writing Your laws upon our hearts. Help us to yield and be changed by Your Word. Please help our spirits and minds embrace the protection of Your covenant. Help us to draw near to You in intimacy and love. Increase our faith so that we live the impossible and experience the miraculous daily. I ask the promise of the Father be sent to each one who is receiving this message by faith and confirm Your Word to them with signs following those who live inside Your covenant.*
>
> *Amen!*

3

Till Death Do
Us Part

It seemed like a match made in Heaven and perhaps it was in the beginning. I was just two weeks shy of my 21st birthday. Sharon (not her real name) and I had grown up in the church. Her parents were my youth pastors. I loved hanging out at their house during the week and playing games. Sharon and I both felt called to vocational ministry. We had the support of our pastor and it was a textbook decision for a couple like us. I had a small business before we were married, and we enjoyed growing our family together. Three years later we had our first child, and I was a proud papa of my son. Two years later we had our second child, this time a daughter.

We received an invitation to plant a church in East Texas. We were both inexperienced about life and especially church planting. Since we were eager to obey the leading of the Holy Spirit, we launched out into the deep, and it certainly was over our heads for sure. The church began to grow and it appeared everything we did was blessed. A couple of years into living in East Texas our third child arrived, a daughter.

Soon after our new arrival, we experienced our first battle and what seemed like a huge betrayal to Sharon. There were three women in the church who were far more experienced in life than Sharon was, and they had taken her in and included her in their activities. I was happy she had found support among some women in the church. Little did we know the plan was for their husbands, who were strong businessmen in the community, to become self-appointed elders. I resisted their maneuvers by suggesting we pray and allow the Holy Spirit to decide who the elders would be. This brought about manipulation from their wives to get my wife to change my mind. They soon rejected her for standing with me. Their actions so wounded Sharon that she wanted nothing to do with ministry or the church.

We stayed another year after that confrontation. The church was still healthy and the effects of the three couples' actions were minimal on the church—but not on Sharon. She told me that she wanted to return home to our families so our children could grow up around their grandparents. She said, "I can't stay here any longer." The toil of a newborn and the rejection of her friends were more than she could bear. I knew my family was more important than a ministry, so we left the church in capable hands and returned to our hometown. I went to work for my father-in-law who wanted to help us get settled after being gone for three years.

AFRICA ENCOUNTER

I had been invited to go to Africa and minister in three different countries and the tickets were already purchased. Sharon agreed that I should go since it would be a waste not to use the tickets. While in Africa the Lord met with the ministry team regularly, we were seeing some of the most powerful demonstrations of the Holy Spirit I had ever experienced. We witnessed confrontations with regional demons that were controlling local officials and saw their wives freed and filled with the Holy Spirit.

On my return, during a stopover in London, I experienced an overshadowing of the Holy Spirit. The room filled up with the presence of God. I heard the Lord say inside my heart, "The enemy has desired to take you out of action and sift your family." Then He said to me, "You will not hear from Me for a while, but know that I am with you; and when you come out of this wilderness, you will come out in the power of the Spirit" (see Luke 4:14). I was not sure why this was happening because we had been witnessing some amazing displays of God's power and now all of a sudden nothing.

When I returned home I was greeted with subdued feelings. Sharon told me some of the things that had taken place while I was away, and she had decided a different course for her life. The months following I was probably more in denial than functioning in reality. She later chose to move out and be on her own so she would not be accountable to anyone else including her family.

The denial soon became reality as I found myself alone with three small children, the youngest still in diapers. I returned to East Texas where I had a job offer. The word to me in Africa came to pass. I did not hear from the Lord for three years, but I knew I had a covenant with God that He would not leave me or forsake me.

I was so helpless at being Mr. Mom. I did not know how to cook much or do laundry. One day I called my mother to tell her something was wrong with the washing machine because the clothes were coming out pinkish. She asked, "Did you separate the colored clothes from the whites?" *Why would I want to do that?* I wondered. Occasionally I saw people who had been in our ministry, and they would encourage me to get back into pastoring. I would always tell them, "I am pastoring…and their names are Kevin, Kristen, and Kara. I prayed daily without sensing anything from the Lord, but I held on to the word I had received in London.

After three years praying and believing for the restoration of the covenant I made ten years previous, Sharon in a very kind manner explained to me that I needed to move on—that she had given birth to other children.

PERSECUTED FOR FAITH'S SAKE

Texas law at that time required we go to court to establish custodial rights for our three children. The attorney opposing me was angry at God and loved the sport of debate. I read in my Bible that morning that I was not to take forethought as to what I would say, but that the Holy Spirit would give me the words to say when it was time to speak. I was comforted with that.

The first question I was asked: "Would you mind speaking in tongues for the court?" I looked at my attorney to do the Perry Mason thing and object to the question, but he looked like a deer staring into headlights.

Then all of a sudden it poured out. I said, "I am sorry I can't speak in tongues for the court."

"Why not?" he asked.

I said, "I can't cast my pearls before swine." Quoting Scripture did not impress him because he was unaware of that verse. I was shocked at myself, but I had not taken thought ahead of time and had never even used that quotation before. There were two long days of grilling about what I believed as the lawyer tried to prove that I would be unfit to raise the children in that kind of environment. It was the happiest day in memory when I took my children home with me. Today they are adults, married with their own children.

My faith was tested but not denied. Later that year I was driving home after conducting an audit in a store where I was the sales manager when all of a sudden I heard the voice of the Lord. It was not audible in the car, but it was loud in my spirit. After three years of living on His covenant promises without any feeling at all, tears filled my eyes like I had just heard from a long lost friend. He said, "It is time to come out from among the stuff" (see 1 Sam. 10:22). There had been invitations to minister during this period, but I declined not knowing whether I would preach again. The Lord impressed me to, "Take the last invitation you received to minister."

As I stood up to share this word in church, someone else stood and gave me this word: "This day the Lord has brought you out of the wilderness in the power of the Holy Spirit." Only I knew the word was exactly what had been given to me in the beginning of the test.

A year later I met Diane, who happened to be Kristen's first grade teacher. I had seen her at some of my meetings; and after a year of enjoying conversation about the goodness of God, we were married. Oh yes, I forgot to mention that she was Miss Texas. God is so faithful to His promises if we just refuse to fall away from what He said He would do. As of this writing Diane and I have been married twenty-five years and are both pastors at Trinity Fellowship in Tyler, Texas.

COVENANTS AND CONSEQUENCES UPON FAMILIES

I still believe that God honors covenants we make. Broken covenants can have consequences that affect generations to come. When there is chronic family dispute and constant drama being played out among siblings, there is a good possibility a breach in covenant could have opened to the harassment. It could be a broken covenant in business or perhaps in marriage or farther back in parents who had been unfaithful. Once the broken covenant is identified, gather everyone around who may be affected and repent to one another, asking the Lord to restore the protection and peace that comes through covenant covering.

For instance, in Second Samuel 12:8-10, after David had restored the unity between Judah and Israel and the ark of God was back in Jerusalem, David became somewhat complacent and was no longer leading his army into war. This is the time when he took Bathsheba from her husband Uriah and had him killed. David breached God's boundaries and stepped over the lines. When Nathan the prophet uses a parable to confront David about the broken covenant, Nathan tells David: after all God has given you if that had been too little, He would have added to you even more things. Because you took the sword and struck down Uriah, the sword will not depart from your house; and I will raise up evil against you from your own household and I will take your wives and give them to your companion (see 2 Sam. 12:8-11).

David brought judgment to his own house because he despised the promise that God would grant him favor and prosperity. David, becoming lax with all his wealth, overstepped God's boundaries and division rose up in his own house. David even had to flee for his own life for a season.

Time and finances have been wasted and lost because heads of households did not take seriously God's laws. I am thankful for the law of grace, which does not replace the law of reaping and sowing. I am thankful for the law of sowing and reaping as well, because we sow to righteousness and reap its rewards. Do we mock God when we willfully choose to step outside of His dominion in our life?

COVENANTS AND CONSEQUENCES UPON THE LAND

Second Samuel 21:1 says, *"There was a famine in the days of David for three years, year after year; and David sought the presence of the Lord. And the Lord said, 'It is for Saul and his bloody house, because he put the Gibeonites to death.'"* The Gibeonites were not even Jews, they were of the Amorites. The Gibeonites deceived Israel into making a covenant with them by posing to be a weak, distant people. But Saul disregarded the covenant he had made with the Gibeonites and slaughtered them.

The consequences showed up later on the land through drought. David called on the Gibeonites to atone for the broken covenant that brought about the curse on the land (see 2 Sam. 21:3). The Gibeonites requested seven sons from Saul's house to be brought to them to be hanged. David did as was requested and they hung in the mountain until the harvest rain.

COVENANT RESTORES HONOR

David had made an oath to Saul's son Jonathan; and when David ruled over Israel, he looked for someone he could show kindness to for the sake of the oath he had made to Jonathan. There was one brought to him named Mephibosheth (see 2 Sam. 9:1). He was crippled in his feet due to being dropped while flee-ing during battle. David brought Mephibosheth to his table and honored him. Mephibosheth was so ashamed that he referred to himself as a dead dog. The curse that was on Saul had brought great shame to his descendants. Mephibosheth had been living outside of the honor that God intended for him. He was living in Lo-debar, which means pasture-less. If there had not been an oath between David and Jonathan, the life of Mephibosheth would have been shameful.

If there had not been a New Covenant between God and His Son, our lives would be without honor and full of shame. If you are reading this and identifying with the shame of Mephibosheth, you can be awakened right now. David went looking for Mephibosheth and he found him. Jesus has covenant promises for you today, and He is looking for you to bring you to His table and wipe away the shame of the past—you are a son or daughter worth every bit of the blood He gave to redeem His Bride.

COVENANT PROMISES TO EXTENDED FAMILY

In Genesis 18:17-19 the Lord says to Abraham, *"Shall I hide from Abraham what I am about to do, since Abraham will surely become a great and mighty nation, and in him all the nations of the earth will be blessed? For I have chosen him, so that he may command his children and his household after him to keep the way of the Lord by doing righteousness and justice...."* This is an incredible statement about God's choices. He chose Abraham because he would command or direct his children to follow the covenant that God gave to him.

God so honored His covenant that He could not proceed with His plans to destroy Sodom and Gomorrah due to the perversion. How would you like to have insider information as to what God was getting ready to do? Abraham's nephew, Lot, was living in Sodom where his soul had become indifferent to the perversion that was happening around him. Genesis 19:29 gives this wonderful insight into God's familial promise to Abraham, *"God remembered Abraham and sent Lot out of the midst of the overthrow* [of Sodom], *when He overthrew the cities in which Lot lived."* Notice it wasn't anything on Lot's part that brought about his and his family's escape. Their rescue was due to the covenant that God had made with Abraham. The angel was sent to escort Lot and his family from Sodom and found resistance on their part to leave. They kept delaying the departure and trying to negotiate with the angel. In verse 22 an angel says, *"Hurry, escape there [Zoar], for I cannot do anything until you arrive there."*

I don't know about you, but this speaks to me that God's wrath was held back until the promise to Abraham was honored. Just think how powerful the New Covenant is that we have through the blood of Jesus. If God did this for Abraham, I believe He will do it for us too. He will send out to our family opportunities to rescue them from the wrath to come. It is in God's mind that none should perish but everyone will come to repentance (see 2 Peter 2:9).

COVENANT PROMISE: YOU ARE THE LORD MY GOD WHO HEALS ME

The following is an account of a pastor's wife who contended for the promise of healing.

> My husband and I participated in a mission trip to India. Though my husband has made many trips to other nations, this was my first time traveling that far from home. I knew that I was about to begin one of the greatest adventures of faith, ministering to those in a far away land. However, I was not aware that my faith would be for life and death for myself.
>
> When we arrived in India, I was not feeling very well because my blood pressure was elevated, and the medication I was taking was having no apparent affect. My training as a nurse caused me to be acutely aware of my predicament. A few days after arriving, I felt a little pressure in my chest. I was trying to gain some relief by resting, staying cool, and praying. I didn't want to

tell my husband, but I knew I needed to because I had a quadruple bypass nine years before. My husband knows I am not a complainer and so he moved into serious prayer mode after I told him. In fact he stayed up all night praying and checking on me. He received a word from the Lord that I would live and not die, and we began to declare and confess that promise while at the same time my condition was getting worse with more chest pressure, neck pain, nausea, and general malaise. I felt very weak and didn't know what to do as the next day we were scheduled to fly farther south into India.

After much prayer my husband decided we needed to make plans to return home as soon as possible. I did not want to go to a local hospital in case my condition was very serious. As we started planning the quick return, the hand of God was with us at precisely the time we needed help. We were able to Skype my son, even though there was a twelve-hour time difference, and we asked him to book tickets immediately. There wasn't Wi-Fi in the hotel room, so we had to sit in a very hot hotel lobby and try to hear him over the noise of a crowd and street traffic. It was about 7 p.m. in the evening, yet my son found tickets to fly us back at 3:30 the next morning.

The next 24 hours would be critical while we were preparing to make the long trip back. We were trusting Jesus as my covenant Healer to keep from going into cardiac arrest. God gave us favor on the flight and connecting flights with seats that allowed us to stretch our legs, which helped prevent blood clots. I was exhausted from my blood pressure and being awake so long, but even though I have never been able to sleep sitting up, the Lord sustained me, and I was able to rest and stay calm. I cried when I felt the love of my husband's concern and care for me. He quoted Scriptures over me, and we remembered the prophetic words that had been spoken to us by Pastor Kerry at our church. The Lord had spoken to us that, "We would finish our race running. And we would have to stand and believe on every promise to be fulfilled that we hadn't seen come to pass." We knew that this was one of those times when we would have to believe in God's promise because there was no help 35,000 feet in the air flying over 20 hours.

We went straight to the ER. They gave me a heart catheter and put in two stents and sent me home to rest. I was to return in a few weeks to have other stents. They had to wait to finish because I had a huge hematoma in my groin due to a pseudo aneurysm in the vessel that was painful and had to stop the bleeding first.

A few days later, the chest and neck pressure began again and I was admitted for another heart catheter and had three more stents placed in the same area to help deal with blockage. Believe it or not I never had a heart attack and there was no damage to my heart. Three days later the pressure and neck pain began again and my cardiologist was stumped. They gave me another heart catheter in the other groin and found that all my vessels were clear. During the treatment, in a routine portion, I suddenly had severe pain shooting up in my abdomen and my blood pressure dropped to 50/20. They started life saving measures and called a surgeon. Meanwhile I was calling on the name of Jesus.

They found that I had a rare type of internal bleeding and the condition required immediate surgery; but as they wheeled me to CCU our King Jesus supernaturally clotted it. Understand that even though I had lost two pints of blood up inside me, they didn't have to do surgery or give me blood. There were several other physical conditions that required medical attention, but regardless the Lord healed me.

My husband and I kept standing on the word, and today I am healed. I am off of all blood pressure medicine and my vessels are open. Jesus is awesome. He has plans for me. Ten weeks later I was able to go on a mission trip to Guatemala. That is our Covenant God.
—Julie Batchelor

This testimony from Julie and her husband demonstrates that God is THE God who keeps covenant and mercy to them who believe Him. They remembered the covenant promises that the Lord had given to them over their lives; and in times of difficulty, they strengthened their spirits by confessing and praying through them.

In times when our faith is being tested with the natural mind, we can panic and begin to question, *Why me?* Psalm 34:15 says, *"The eyes of the Lord are toward the righteous and His ears are open to their cry."* The key here is being in the right place of covenant with God. To be righteous could be said is to be under His dominion and there His eyes are toward us and He hears those in covenant. Especially at 35,000 feet, I want to be covered with His righteousness.

THE SIGN OF THE SECURITY

One of the signs of covenant that I learned as a child was the importance of security in a stable home. A marriage is not only about a husband and wife when there are children involved. When the marriage is secure, the children see love expressed, they feel secure, and are more apt to perform their best at whatever they do in school.

You know what I craved as a kid growing up? I couldn't tell you why then, but I craved to see my mother and dad kiss in front of us. It may sound strange to you, but love expressed was rare unless my mother was the initiator. When I went to our neighbor's house and saw their parents show affection, it made me feel secure. I wanted to see my mom and dad do the same. Unfortunately, my parents weren't as openly affectionate around us. My mother would say, "Do you love me?" and my dad would say, "You know I do, if I change my mind I'll let you know."

God is all about wanting to express His love for us. Perhaps that is why the Bible teaches so much about worship. Worship is not to be bottled up. In fact, we were created to express worship in spirit and truth. The more we are free to give expression to His adoration, the more we feel secure in the covenant He has given to us.

I believe that when we are in covenant, God will make our homes such sanctuaries that neighbors will come over and say, "I don't know what you're doing, but your kids are so peaceful and well-behaved."

The great theologian, Andrew Murray says this:

> In entering into covenant with us, God's one object is to draw us to Himself, to render us entirely dependent upon Himself, and so to bring us into the right position and disposition in which He can fill us with Himself, His love, and His blessedness. Let us undertake our study of the New Covenant, in which, if we are believers, God is at this moment living and walking with us, with the honest purpose and surrender, at any price, to know what God wishes to be to us, to

do in us, and to have us be and do to Him. The New Covenant may become to us one of the windows of heaven through which we see into the face, into the very heart, of God.

COVENANT TRANSFORMS OUR MINDS AND POSITIONS

Understanding covenant requires that we embrace the imagination or mind of God and what He has called us to be in Christ. We have to let go of who we think we are, who others say we are and allow the Spirit to renew our minds and spirits with what God has called us to be. Jesus asked the disciples, "Who do they say I am?" In the same manner, and with a listening spirit, every person must ask, "Lord, who do YOU say I am?"

In Ephesians, Paul exhorts the believers and explains the incredible position that God has placed us in:

> *But God who is rich in mercy, for his great love wherewith he loved us, even when we were dead in sins, hath quickened us together with Christ,* (by grace ye are saved) *and hath rraised us up together, and made us sit together in heavenly places in Christ Jesus* (Ephesians 2:4-6 KJV).

Paul goes on to describe the joy that the Lord has in us: *"For we are his workmanship, created in Christ Jesus unto good works, which God hath before ordained that we should walk in them"* (Eph. 2:10 KJV).

Next Paul reminds us of where we were before God's covenant:

> *Wherefore remember, that ye being in time past Gentiles in the flesh, who are called Uncircumcision by that which is called the Circumcision in the flesh made by hands; that at that time ye were without Christ, being aliens*

from the commonwealth of Israel, and strangers from the covenants of promise, having no hope, and without God in the world: But now in Christ Jesus ye who sometimes were far off are made nigh by the blood of Christ. For he is our peace, who hath made both one, and hath broken down the middle wall of partition between us (Ephesians 2:11-14 KJV).

When we consider what other religions say their gods want from them, this loving and paternal attitude is of magnanimous proportions. Paul provides a paradigm shift of incredible proportions to what has been humanity's relationship to gods in the past. Holding the thoughts that "We are seated in high places with Christ" with being "God's workmanship," it reflects on the power and impact that being in covenant with a living God can have. It makes our relationship with the Lord vital, real, and expansive. God wants us to have more than a better understanding of covenant; He wants us to operate in all of the benefits of covenant that the Lord intended.

Jesus paid a huge price by establishing covenant for us and in us. He wants us to embrace His power, grace, and joy in the New Covenant so that we are transformed and celebrating in the exciting destiny that the Lord has for each of us. The New Covenant is not only what Jesus did for us 2,000 years ago, but even now how He is transforming us to fit into His master plan.

Lord Jesus,

Open our hearts to be free to express the love connection we have with You. May we never be ashamed of coming to Your table to eat Your bread. You are the true bread that gives life. Give us this day daily bread that may sustain us forever. May the Lord grant you a marriage that is truly a covenant built on the foundation of Christ! May your children be secure in your love for each other. Let each person reading this prayer find faith to raise him or her to a new level of confidence in You, Lord. We know in whom we believe and we are persuaded to keep what we have committed to You against the end of the age. May the peace of God rule every part of your life and know His eye truly is upon you.

Amen!

4

THE IMPACT OF COVENANT

---◆---

I N THE NEW Testament there is another word that expresses covenant in a different application—*diatheke*—meaning the stronger of the two parties involved in a covenant; in which case, the weight of responsibility for fulfilling the agreement falls on the stronger. In the *diatheke* type, the covenant is not made based on the recipients but solely on the strength of the one who is the guarantor. In a business type of contract, if there is one whose credit is not strong enough, he or she could ask another to be a co-signer. The co-signer signs alongside of the one purchasing the property, but the co-signer bears the responsibility to pay for anything the signer is unable to pay. Though the signer receives all the benefits of the loan, the co-signer takes all liability and possible blame for the contract. When the bank or mortgage company looks at the contract, they look solely at the guarantor, who bears the weight of the contract and all of its penalties. Remember in Exodus 12 when God told the Hebrews to put the blood over the doorposts before judgment came upon Egypt. He said, "When I see the blood I will pass over you." The blood was the co-signer for the house. Those in the house were not worthy to pay the price for their freedom.

We all are debtors without the ability to pay for the sin we were born into. God sent His guarantor, His Son Jesus. He was our *Diatheke* who was stronger. He overcame the devil and death. He signed the covenant in His own blood. We don't have to worry about any repossession of His property.

Paul the apostle said in First Corinthians 6:19-20:

> *Do you not know that your body is a temple of the Holy Spirit who is in you, whom you have from God, and that you are not your own? For you have been bought with a price: therefore glorify God in your body.*

The only the requirement of this *diatheke* covenant is for me to believe in my heart and confess with my mouth that Jesus is my resurrected Lord. My part is small, without comparison for all He has done. We have tremendous power and authority when we consider the backing we have to succeed in this life. Our co-signer has already signed in blood and has given us the right to use His name. When He said, "Let my will be done on earth as it is Heaven," He gave us the covenant power to enforce His purpose over the devil and bring freedom to all who call upon His name from sincere hearts.

In our marriage to Jesus, He certainly has laid down His life for us when we were dead in trespasses. We could not do anything to help ourselves. Then the *Diatheke* took our place and gave us the deed to what He paid for.

This kind of covenant is also viewed as the last will and testament. This is the legal instrument used in which inheritances are conveyed from one generation to the next. The estate is transferred to the heirs through a will or a testament. All of the wishes of the person owning the estate are placed in the will. The promises are spelled out there including how the assets will be distributed. The will is irrevocable and cannot be altered except by the one who has made the promises. Hebrews 9 describes this process: Jesus through His own blood and through the eternal Spirit offered Himself and became the mediator of a new covenant (see Heb. 9:15). Hebrews 9:17 says a covenant is valid only when men are dead, and without the shedding of blood there is no forgiveness.

Jesus died so we would inherit His estate, and the assets He has left us are never consumed but continue to be distributed forever. In Acts 1:4 Jesus told His followers to go to Jerusalem and wait for the promise of the Father. I have the picture in my mind as if the family was gathered in the office of a Judge waiting for the last Will and Testament of their departed father to be read. Then suddenly a sound no one could describe filled the room. Some were waiting to hear what their part of the inheritance would be, but instead they were all filled with the Holy Spirit. Everything changed from that moment on. They were no longer looking for silver and gold but were astonished at the love that suddenly invaded their lives. They started speaking in new tongues while they looked at one another and saw tongues of fire hovering over each other. Now they understood the promise of the Father they were looking for was part of Himself now residing inside them.

We have an inheritance that is far greater than anything we could imagine because it is not a temporary blessing but rather eternal in value. Please don't devalue the wealth that you are in Christ. You are the recipient of His Will and Testament.

If you are feeling helpless and overwhelmed with life and are hoping someone will stand up for you, I can tell you without a shadow of a doubt that Christ Jesus is the one who will stand beside you closer than a brother. Even with all the mistakes and piles of past baggage, right now let Him enter your domain and take dominion of your life. He will place a no trespassing seal signed in His blood that the devil cannot cross over. Let Him lift the cares of life from you at this very moment. He wants to comfort and heal you.

THE WEIGHT OF COVENANT

Perhaps the best-known type of covenant is the one found in Genesis 15. God promises Abraham a son who will come from his own body. You may remember that Abraham assumed it was his responsibility to come up with his own heir, so he chose a faithful servant, Eliezer. God wanted Abraham to get the picture in his mind of the magnitude God would do through this promise of his son. (For more detail, read my book *The Power of Imagination.*) God wanted Abraham to see this promise would affect not only him and his descendants, but all the families of the earth would be connectors to this covenant.

Abraham asks a sincere question of God that many of us ask in similar ways. In Genesis 15:8 Abraham asks, *"O Lord God, how may I know that I will possess it?"* He wanted something from God that he could stand on as a promise or perhaps like a contract. He already believed God was Jehovah. The issue was the claim ticket. How may I possess it? What will give Abraham ownership of the promise that a son is coming, realizing both he and Sarah were beyond the natural ability to produce children?

In Genesis 15:9 is a remarkable picture of how we enter into covenant today. God instructed Abraham to take various animals, cut them in two, and lay each half opposite the other half. After Abraham obeyed God's instructions, a deep sleep from the Lord came upon him; and while in his sleep God speaks to Abraham an incredible prophetic word concerning his future generations.

Then all of a sudden there appeared two objects passing between the sacrifices Abraham had prepared. One object was a smoking oven and the other was a flaming torch. The torch is a symbol of Christ representing the Son. The Bible describes Christ as the light of the world that will reveal God the Father. The oven symbolizes the refiner's oven or furnace of affliction and testing. The torch speaks more of the New Covenant, when the light will break forth as the dawn. The smoking oven represents God the Father and more of the Old Covenant where the Ten Commandments tested the hearts of the people and the wilderness was testing the Hebrews coming out of Egypt.

The most exciting part of this picture is seeing the Father and the Son passing between the sacrifices making covenant. Since the beginning of time humankind has been found to be a covenant breaker. The first Adam did not live in the covenant God had given him in Eden. Because man cannot keep covenant, the Father makes covenant with His Son the Torch that whosoever believes in Him the Father will receive into the Kingdom of Heaven. The New Covenant is actually a covenant between God the Father and God the Son. The redeeming price was the blood of the Son.

Abraham prepared the sacrifice, but the covenant was made in behalf of him—not made through him. I am so thankful that the New Covenant that enables us to possess the promises of God was not given through a man. Jesus, the Second Adam, overcame everything the first Adam failed in. The first Adam failed in the Garden of Eden; Jesus the Second Adam overcame in His garden of Gethsemane. We have a sure foundation to ask in the name of our Covenant Redeemer with an expectation of His response.

THE SIGN OF KABOD

In times of trial or difficulty, one of the most quoted passages of Scripture is:

No temptation has overtaken you but such as is common to man; and God is faithful, who will not allow you to be tempted beyond what you are able, but with the temptation will provide the way of escape also, so that you will be able to endure it (1 Corinthians 10:13).

This verse is used many times as an escape hatch out of a problem. Usually only half of the verse is quoted—especially the part about God not putting on us any more than we can bear.

———◆———

One day while on my way to a meeting where I was going to be speaking, I sensed the Holy Spirit prompting this verse to me but emphasizing it in a way I had never heard before. I heard it like this, "I will not put any more of Myself on you than you can bear." It hit me squarely between the eyes. The Holy Spirit started taking me to other portions of Scripture to validate what I was hearing. For instance, Moses, in Exodus 33, asks God to show him His glory. Moses had already experienced more supernatural demonstrations of God than anyone in history. He saw the enemies of the Hebrews swallowed in the sea by God's power—and now if that is not enough, he wants more. After dealing with all the logistical problems associated with leading two million complaining people across the desert, miracles were not enough anymore. Moses wanted to personally know God, not just His power.

God begins the negotiating by saying, "My presence will go with you." Moses replies that he doesn't want to proceed with God's presence. Finally the full question comes from Moses, "Show me Your glory" (see Exod. 33:19). God explains to Moses no one can live and look on the face of God. Just think of the radiation that would emanate from that intensity of glory. The desire of Moses touches the heart of God and the request is granted. God tells him that He has to put Moses into the right place in order for him to receive God's glory. There was a place in the rock where Moses could stand and God would cover him with His hand (see Exod. 33:21-22).

We know that place to be a prophetic picture of Jesus the Rock of Ages. Only in Christ can any of us experience the presence of God and through the covenant of the Son can we see the glory of God.

Perhaps you feel exhausted as you continue to believe for some type of change to come into your life. Right now you can ask the same thing Moses did—to be covered by the hand of God so the glory of God can pass by. One moment in His glory changes everything. The word for glory in Exodus 33:19 is *kabod*, literally meaning weightiness. God described His glory to Moses as His goodness. Pure goodness passing by so lit up Moses to the point it was shining through on his face.

I realize the verse in First Corinthians refers also to testing. God will not put on us any more than we can bear, right? Since God wants us to be carriers of His presence and we are called a temple of God, then perhaps the testing is to prepare us for a weightier *(kabod)* measure of Him. In Luke 6:46-49, Jesus is sharing a parable about those who hear the word and respond in faith and those who don't. He uses the analogy of a person building a house. One who is wise will take the necessary time to prepare. The wise will dig deep and lay a foundation, and the unwise will not. Notice the same testing of wind and flood came on both houses; the wise didn't escape the testing. The distinction was made clear resulting in one house standing strong and the other being utterly destroyed. The one who heard the word and acted upon it passed the test and was said to be wise.

The purpose of the testing was not to fail anyone but to reveal the house that was ready for the weightiness of God's favor. The great thing about tests when it comes to covenant is that we get to keep taking them until we pass. He is in charge of the testing for the purpose of graduating us, not failing us. Do you want more of His presence in your life?

This idea of testing is similar to a building inspector. The inspector is there not to make the lives of the builder miserable but to ensure quality and safety. Once the inspector says the foundation is correct, then the walls can go up. When the first floor passes the test and has shown it can carry the weight of another floor, then the next phase can begin. The Holy Spirit comes as an inspector and watches over the plans being laid in our lives, and He can speed things up or He can slow them down or even stop them.

Jesus was using this same concept when speaking to some Pharisees in Luke 19:44. Jesus said there would not be one stone left upon another *"because you did not recognize the time of your visitation."* The word for visitation *(episkope)* is interesting because it means to inspect. Jesus was saying to them, "You should have recognized I was here to inspect the work." The inspection proved to be a visit when they didn't receive His Word and the veil remained over their eyes to blind them of the promise of the Father.

The last part of the familiar verse in First Corinthians is the part about escape. We like that part because along with the testing there comes an escape. In my mind I always pictured a special escape hatch, so right before I buckled under the weight of the problem, God would push a button and the escape hatch would open up and a giant slide would appear and take me out of the crisis. The word escape simply means the exit or the end of the testing. When I had to take tests in school I was always glad when the escape, the end, was in sight.

I think we should also balance this out with what James 1:13 says, *"Let no one say when he is tempted, 'I am being tempted by God'; for God cannot be tempted by evil, and He Himself does not tempt anyone."* So if God doesn't tempt or test us, then why does the Bible say, "Count it all joy when you fall into various trials, knowing that the testing of your faith produces endurance"? (See James 1:2-3.)

There is a difference between temptation and testing. In verses 14 and 15 James says, *"Each one is tempted when he is carried away and enticed by his own lust. Then when lust has conceived, it gives birth to sin; and when sin is accomplished, it brings forth death."* Testing prepares us for the *kabod* of God, but temptation is when there is that crooked place of lust in us that leans in the direction of the old Adam. The new Adam is being formed after the image of Christ and is a habitation that will be strong enough to carry the *kabod* of glory.

The pain and suffering of humanity was placed upon Jesus. He took the weight of the world so we could receive the weight of His glory. However, we as carriers of His weightiness must grow, being able to carry His goodness.

In Psalm 105, it says that the Word of the Lord tested Joseph. Though Joseph had a dream that perhaps would help keep him moving forward in his destiny, he had to continue to trust God that the dream was his promise. When we embrace a prophetic declaration or covenant directive from the Lord, there is a time of transition before the promise becomes a reality. Just like the seed must die before the plant grows, we experience the pain of change before the promise comes to pass. Faith helps us make sure we are in alignment to realize the covenant promise we are standing for.

If Joseph had come to his ultimate place ahead of time, he may not have had the experience to rule at the level God intended. I wonder how many times we settle for less than God's intentions because we aborted the testing of the word we received many years prior. Part of trusting God for the outcome of things is leaving the timing to Him. If we regularly go and dig up the seed to see if there has been any change, will our curiosity delay the process? Just trust the inspection of the Holy Spirit that there is more happening in our lives than what we know.

Joseph may have had days while in the prison when he wondered why his life turned out that way; however, we don't get that picture from the Bible. Everywhere Joseph was placed he rose to the top and took the opportunity to do the best with the gifts God gave him. Then one day Joseph was ready; his gift had matured and the two came together. When the promise of God and the timing of God intersect, there is a "suddenly." The suddenly for your life may seem to all of a sudden appear, but the truth is you have been moving on that trajectory for a while, and the time and the season were being watched over because you are in covenant.

The covenant with Abraham was still in affect working through Joseph. While Abraham was asleep and God was speaking during the covenant to be enacted, He told Abraham that his people would be in a strange land where they would be enslaved and oppressed for four hundred years, but afterward they would come out with many possessions (see Gen. 15:13-14). The dream that Joseph had was a continuation of the covenant God had with Abraham. My point here is you are part of a bigger plan than just finding your way in life. God is having His way in and through your life, fulfilling a New Covenant. Once we resign ourselves to being part of the giant plan of covenant, the easier it is to see how things work together for our good.

Romans 8:28 is a favorite verse of some who use it to explain why things happen the way they do. It says, *"God causes all things to work together for good to those who love God, to those who are called according to His purpose."* There are two prerequisites for this Scripture to fit the "all things are good" usage. The first is that we must love God. That seems elementary—no problem there, or is there? To love God means more than having feelings for Him. Jesus said, *"If you love Me, you will keep My commandments"* (John 14:15). He defines love as demonstrated through obedience to God's Word. In that sense we can only say that all things work together for good only for those who are adhering to the Word of God. Hang on a moment, there is more to the verse.

The second criterion is to be called according to His purpose. The purpose of God is not that you have to become a preacher, but that you want the same things as He does. For instance He doesn't want any to perish but for everyone to come to the knowledge of the Son of God, which takes us back to His Covenant. So now we can say if we are obedient to His Word, which shows I love Him and I want the same things in purpose, then I can claim that all things are working in our lives for good. The outcome is going to be good because it is framed by a covenant that is bigger than one person or one generation. The exciting part for me—and for all of God's children—is that I can be part of that eternal plan called the New Covenant—so can you!

> *Lord Jesus, would You give us Your glory. Allow every person reading this chapter to see themselves as part of Your plan. If the devil has blinded and detoured them, I ask for them to be led back to the place in the Rock where they are covered with Your presence. Help us to recognize that You have a suddenly planned for us and we are on track to run across the timing of the Holy Spirit. I pray for those who are discouraged or disappointed, whose plans have not been fulfilled; today give them a new set that have been drawn by the Creator of the universe. Give them dreams and night visions so they might hope again. You really do*

have a hope and a future for us that are according to Your purpose. I ask that the readers of this prayer will find the purpose of their covenant connection.

In Jesus' name,

Amen!

5

SURPRISED BY
HIS BLESSINGS

———◆———

I T WAS A lesson I needed to learn, and the Holy Spirit has unique ways to make the point. I had become increasingly busy, and the days seemed to run together. I was starting to think increased activity produced increased productivity. But I was soon to find out differently.

It happened on one of those days when I least expected it. I thought I had my day mapped out and in place when my secretary told me my two o'clock appointment was coming. I replied, "I don't have an appointment scheduled." She apologized and took the responsibility for the slip-up. When I asked who was scheduled to meet with me, she strangely said, "I'm not sure." Before I could quiz her anymore, she turned and left my office.

I had about half an hour before the unscheduled appointment was to arrive. I continued working on my project, and then my wife, Diane, stepped into my office. I said, "Hi, Babe, how is your day? I have a two o'clock appointment any moment now." She said, "Yes, I know, I'm your two o'clock."

I think the blood drained out of my face and had the sudden thought, *I'm in over my head.* She smiled and asked me how my day was going and I haltingly said ok. She never gave her hand away as to what the unexpected visit was about. Finally I felt like the little boy going to the principal's office. I was searching my memory banks asking myself if I could have forgotten an important date. While still smiling she said, "I just wanted to see you. We have not had much time with all the changes in scheduling, so I thought we could take a few minutes and just chat about anything you want."

I was for the first time without much to say. I was captured by her desire to be with me. So much so she was willing to make an appointment. The message came through loud and clear. I asked her to forgive me because I had substituted being together with being busy, thinking it was to benefit her and our family. Diane's love language is time. Mine is acts of service. I was giving her what I valued instead of giving what she values, and in this case it was time with me. The covenant that I have with my wife still needs to be nourished with time together even after twenty-five years of marriage.

TIME FOR COVENANT

It may be hard to think in terms of Jesus wanting to be with us, after all He is God—He doesn't need anything. On the contrary, He has allowed Himself to want to be with us. When celebrating the last Passover meal with His disciples, Jesus said, "I have earnestly desired to eat this Passover with you" (see Luke 22:15). As if that is not enough, we are told that as often as we take the Lord's Table (participate in a Communion service), we remember Him. I certainly don't want the Lord to have to make an appointment to have time with me. I am the one who benefits from His encounter.

Any counselor or sociologist would tell us that we make time for what we value. If my covenant in marriage or in my covenant relationship with Christ is just assumed, then when I am in need, the benefits of the covenant will be there. It is true that Jesus will never leave us nor forsake us. He doesn't divorce us. When the truth of covenant is in the center of a home and marriage, there is a sense of security and peace. But in order to build and maintain covenant in relationships, it is critical to spend time together. This is how we continue to understand each other.

The same is true with our relationship with the Lord. The covenant was revealed on tablets and stones on the outward, but the New Covenant that is ratified through the blood of Jesus, is now written upon our hearts. We are the circumcision made without hands, because we have received the circumcision of the heart. I am deeply in love with Jesus, and I always feel refreshed and at peace with others when I have been with Him through prayer and worship.

COVENANT CLEAVES, CONTRACTS LEAVE

One of the best examples of this type of covenant is found in the Book of Ruth. When tragedy hit the family and the two sons of Naomi died, the only ones left were two daughters-in-law and their aged mother-in-law. This beautiful history reminds us to never give up when circumstances point to grief and destruction.

Ruth chapter 1 opens with Naomi, whose name means pleasant, telling people to call her Mara, meaning bitter, because she feels God has dealt bitterly with her. Naomi tells her daughters-in-law that they should go back to the place of their birth. Naomi does not encourage them to stay with her. One daughter-in-law, Orpah, which means stubborn, kissed Naomi and returned to her people and her gods. Ruth, however, clung to Naomi even though Naomi tried to discourage her.

Ruth declares these well-known words, "Where you go I will go, where you die I will die, and your people shall be my people." These words have for decades now been recited as vows in wedding ceremonies. I wonder how many couples realize what they are reciting. Ruth, whose name means friend, made a choice not to return to what was a familiar or family past—she would instead cleave to Naomi. Based upon the circumstances, there wasn't any security that Naomi could offer Ruth. As Naomi was also grieving the loss of her husband, they were quite a pair together. The beauty of this story is the set up behind the scenes that would affect the ages to come. On the surface no one could have seen this happy ending coming.

The plan was for Ruth to go into the fields and glean what she could then share it with Naomi. Ruth was truly showing she was a friend. She was a friend who was sticking closer than a brother. She found favor in the field of Boaz who just happened to be a distant relative of Naomi. Boaz notices Ruth and instructs the other field hands not to bother or insult her. Boaz tells her to stay in his field, not to go to another field. Do you notice all the opportunities for Ruth to leave and go home or even go to another field? But she stays close to Naomi. Favor for Ruth increases to the point that Boaz has his gleaners leave handfuls of grain on purpose for Ruth to find.

Doesn't this sound like our Lord? We are invited to come closer and we start seeing handfuls of blessings to help us along the journey. Ruth who had not stopped clinging to Naomi is now in a position for her life to do a 180-degree turn. Naomi instructs Ruth to prepare herself with bathing and her best clothes, then position herself close to Boaz. (I wonder how many opportunities we lost because we didn't want to follow instructions, which kept us out of position to receive.) That evening Boaz realized Ruth was with him and accepts the responsibility to redeem her.

Bible scholars have traced the lineage of Christ and discovered the thread running through the lineage of Ruth. Our Covenant Redeemer is Jesus who paid off our debt and invites us to no longer go into another field—but to stay with Him. He will make sure you have hands full. If you are feeling empty and lonely, you can find a new identity with Jesus. You might know Him in name but never moved close enough to allow Him to spread His garments over you. The feeling of insecurity and being uncovered makes you feel vulnerable. The simplest act of asking Jesus to take your life and make it His own can bring a huge change for you. You could have a shift in your life now as you read this prophetic picture of covenantal love.

GOD WANTS TO BE CLOSE

Throughout history God has desired to be up close and personal with His children. His vision for a people with whom He could interact was His desire from the beginning. Before Adam chose to be independent from God by eating from the forbidden tree, God fellowshipped with Adam and Eve. They knew God and His sound moving in the Garden was the way life was meant to be. They had no shame and no fear—only relationship. Their covering was the glory of God. Adam looked at Eve every day filtered through the glory that was covering their eyes and bodies.

When the fateful day of failure came, they realized things had changed because they were no longer covered by God's presence. Their first response, like many of us, was to hide themselves from the interaction they had always known. Adam sees his wife for the first time without God's covering and she the same with him. They were like orphans not knowing what was to happen next because they had no experience outside of God's glory. God asks them, "Where are you?" Obviously God knew where they were, but I think He wanted them to acknowledge their sin.

Like all sin, it caused them to play the blame game. Adam blamed his wife and Eve blamed the serpent. Neither wanted to take responsibility that they had broken covenant with God—and that's the reason we are to this very day still feeling naked and unsure about tomorrow. But even before that moment when humankind walked away from the covenant of God, God had a plan of redemption to bring us closer to Him.

God promised Abraham that after four hundred years of being enslaved his generations would be brought out of the bondage of Egypt. God wanted to bring His people close to Himself. After seeing all of the amazing miracles that God worked through the hands of Moses, yet the people didn't know this God Moses had introduced them to. They were so ready and willing to exit Egypt they did not have time to inquire who He was. They had some history of the God of Abraham, Isaac, and Jacob. They had heard of the stories of Joseph, but no history lesson brought Jehovah God up close and personal to them.

Upon their exodus, Moses was instructed to bring them to Mount Sinai in the Arabian Desert. There the people saw a mountain that was on fire and the ground shook beneath their feet. God had called Moses to come up and meet with Him. All that the Hebrews knew about God firsthand was that He was war-like. They saw an entire army disposed of in the Red Sea in just a moment of time, and now they saw a God who is on a fiery mountain. This was too much for them as their get-acquainted meeting. They were fine with Moses going up into the mountain and being the representative for God, but they did not want to get any closer.

God was still desirous to move in closer to interact with His covenant people. Due to their distant approach to God the priesthood system was set in place. Moses' brother was selected to be the high priest, and all other priests were to come from the same family. The people, feeling they wanted a less personal god, created one from their past experience that looked like the golden calves in Egypt.

Before we get too judgmental, we should remember the times when many Christians revert to familiar responses and offenses. The golden calf and its idolatry drew the people around something they could control and was created out of their own image. Yet God in His mercy continued with His covenantal plan to draw them close to Himself. The priests were to represent the people to God and thus they were insulated from the presence of God. Much of religion today has a form of godliness, denying the people the right to encounter God for themselves.

In Exodus 25, God instructs Moses to erect a tent, later to be called the tent of meeting or Moses' Tabernacle. This tent would serve to bring God closer to the people. The outer part of the place of meeting was to have an altar made from brass where the sacrifices to God would take place. Anyone could watch the priests work there. Moses was to place inside the tent a holy place and the furniture was to reflect the personality and desire God had for this people. The people were not allowed past the outer court. Only the priests could go inside to the Holy Place and serve.

God wanted to come among the people so He designed a box where His glory would live. Moses was to cover this box that was constructed from gnarly Acacia wood. The difficult wood served to represent the humanity of the people. Moses was to use the gold taken from the Egyptians to cover the box. The top of the box was to be called the Mercy Seat. Two cherubims with wings extended and touching would cover the Mercy Seat. This box was to be called the Ark of the Covenant. God was now closer to the people than He was on Mount Sinai. Only the high priest could enter there once a year and place blood on the Mercy Seat to cover the sins of the nation for the year. In Exodus 25:22 God reveals His heart more clearly:

*There I will meet with you; and from above the **mercy seat**, from between the two cherubim which are upon the ark of the testimony, I will speak to you about all that I will give you in commandment for the sons of Israel.*

God now has come closer than ever before to Israel. He could have chosen many different ways and places to commune with them, but He chose the Mercy Seat. It is still today God's way of meeting with us—through His mercy. It's true He is a God of judgment, but He wants to meet with humankind in this time through mercy. Deuteronomy 7:9 describes God as the faithful one who keeps covenant and mercy. The people were able to see God's presence in the tent of meeting, but were still distant from knowing God up close and personal.

The time came when the promise to inherit the land of Canaan had arrived. Moses was gone and Joshua who had been consistent to linger at the tent of meeting was to lead the nation to their new land. The instructions were simple as to when they were to move. Joshua 3:3 instructs the people, *"When you see the ark of the covenant of the Lord your God with the Levitical priests carrying it, then you shall set out from your place and go after it."*

Israel had learned during their time in the desert that their lives were to center on the covenant. Anything God was doing was going to have the covenant in the center of it. It was simple; keep your eyes upon the Ark of the Covenant and you won't be left out of inheriting the promise.

THE ARK OF BLESSING

The nations that were warring against Israel soon learned they could not defeat the God of Israel. The presence of God was the weapon they relied upon. There came a time when Saul was king and they used the Ark not as holy but like an object of warfare. The Ark had fallen into enemy hands. The enemy quickly discovered that the God of Israel was not favorable to them. David is now finally anointed as king over both Judah and Israel, and his first order of business was to return the Ark of the Covenant to Jerusalem. Because they did not inquire of the Lord as to how to bring the Ark back and used a cart instead of the priests, one man dies. So David stores the Ark in a nearby house, with a guy named Obed-edom, for three months and what a glorious three months it was for this non-Jewish family (see 1 Chron. 13:14). They prospered and were so affected having the Ark of the Covenant in their home that when David came to take the Ark to Jerusalem, all of Obed-edom's household moved and followed the presence of God to Jerusalem.

In Jerusalem, God was now closer to His people and more interactive with them.

Psalm 16:11 says that in the presence of the Lord there is fullness of joy, and at His right hand are pleasures forevermore.

Just think for a moment how wonderful it would be to have the presence of God in your home. Your children would excel in school and favor would be upon Mom and Dad and every-thing you did would be prosperous. We don't need to think too far out of the box, because God has actually left the box—He has provided the Mercy Seat of His Son Jesus. His blood has been placed on the Mercy Seat in Heaven, and we don't have to be distant from Him. In fact, you and I are now the "box" He lives in. We just need to be conscious of His indwelling and not ignore Him. Since the mercy of God lives in us, we are called to be dispensers of that mercy. Truth and Mercy have met, the Bible says. Because we have the truth that is brought by the Holy Spirit and the mercy of the New Covenant, no one can defeat us.

YOKED TOGETHER

Daniel came to me perplexed as to why his wife of fifteen years suddenly wanted out of the marriage. I met with her soon after this happened, and I was surprised at what I heard as well. Mary was well liked in the church, as was Daniel. Neither one had ever voiced a dissatisfaction that would lead anyone outside the home to see this one coming. Mary had become confident and strong enough to voice her feelings. She said, "I feel like I married my father and not my husband." Daniel felt as if he had married a child who was content for him to do everything. She was a quiet young woman when they married and a few years into the marriage she confessed an affair and a child soon followed from the illicit relationship. Daniel continued in the marriage willing to raise the child. He was still seen by Mary as the father type who would fix all of her problems. He was a fix-it kind of a guy who was very reliable. Over the years she matured emotionally but not when it came to her marriage. She now wanted a marriage where two were equally yoked together. Without any more discussion, she abruptly left Daniel with the three boys.

Eventually Daniel met someone else, this time he was more mature and they enjoyed doing things together. The things they did together consisted of Daniel fixing things. His ability to fix things was the attraction. After some counseling, he came to some incredible insights. He said, "You know, Pastor, I discovered I was trying to make a friendship into a covenant relationship." I said to him, "You have unlocked a key for many. There is a difference between a friendship and a covenant relationship such as marriage."

Daniel is now in the process of learning to recognize the difference. He now knows he wants to be loved for who he is and not solely for what he does. Previously Daniel felt comfortable in an unyoked relationship because he was totally in charge and did not have to consider another's input.

Jesus said in Matthew 11:28-29:

> *Come to Me, all who are weary and heavy-laden, and I will give you rest.* **Take My yoke upon you and learn from Me,** *for I am gentle and humble in heart, and you will find rest for your souls.*

A yoke in biblical culture was not uncommon. Jesus used the example to depict the relationship we can have with Him. The word yoke is *zugos,* translated to describe the yoke as two things held together for the purpose of increasing strength. Proverbs tells us two are better than one, in case one falls there is someone to help you get up. Jesus is inviting us to be yoked, connected in such a way that our ability and strength are maximized. There is also the picture of a large animal yoked to a smaller animal—an unequal yoke. The large animal will pull on the smaller and simply drag it around. On the contrary, Jesus says His yoke is easy it will not overpower you. It will bring out the best in you and you won't fail because your strength is made perfect in your weakness. He brings up our weakest to become strength.

The second opportunity we have is to learn of Him. Notice He doesn't say learn about Me but learn from Me. The yoking becomes a covenant at this point not just a friendly banter but instead an intimate encounter that causes us to take on the nature of the one we are yoked to. One paraphrase of this verse is to be printed upon as the learning experience; or in other words, He deeply presses us into His image. We don't get this as casual friends who go their separate ways at the end of the day.

When a marriage becomes laborious, it is an indication that the covenant partners are going in different directions and the yoke is no longer is easy. When the yoke gets uneasy, it is easy for some to think they should get out of the yoke, or marriage. The real issue isn't the yoke; the problem is the commitment to the yoke.

DIFFERENT VOICES IN THE GARDEN

Adam and Eve were given a yoke. It was a covenant that was spelled out for them. It was only when another voice entered into the yoke that confusion and doubt was introduced. It would be the first time that division entered into the yoke. The question? Did God really mean it like that? Maybe He didn't mean we would die. They began to rationalize, *Maybe this yoke is not me anymore and I have outgrown this marriage.* The idea was introduced to Adam; and is not a new tactic for the devil to use on us today. The serpent introduced the idea that God was keeping Adam and Eve from experiencing something. *Is there possibly more I could experience outside of this yoke?*

The devil is still introducing seducing thoughts that the grass may be greener on the other side of your marriage. The devil will do anything to get you to break your yoke and strike out on your own. God honors marriage because after all He invented it. The yoke is the covering that keeps us in God's will. It is not just the yoke of marriage it is a yoke God has given as His plan. God granted divorce because of the hardness of the hearts of the people, not because He was allowing them to find someone more to their liking. Hard hearts bring up the idea of divorce. When people start considering breaking the yoke, they should look closer at their heart. Remember it was God who said man looks on the outward but God looks at the heart.

I know the pain of divorce and what it does to the entire family, yet God is gracious to redeem things we have messed up when we turn toward Him, not away from Him. I am not advocating someone stay in a relationship that may be potentially violent, but most divorces result because the husband and wife have just stopped communicating. If a voice has entered your garden that is opposing the voice of God, you have to make a determination to turn to God and not hide from Him.

If you are finding the yoke binding on your marriage, then please allow the Holy Spirit to renew your love compassion toward your spouse. If you have allowed another voice to enter the sanctity of your covenant, right now stop before reading any farther and ask for forgiveness and for the Covenant Keeper Jesus to cleanse the marriage and give you eyes to see your spouse through God's eyes. Generations may depend upon the decision you make. I don't claim to know your situation, but I do know there is help available if your heart is not hardened.

ENJOYING THE YOKE

James couldn't wait to turn 19 so he could leave home and be on his own. He didn't have a job, but the plan was to live with friends until he could figure it out. He eventually got a job busing tables at a local fast food restaurant, and was then able to rent a rundown add-on to the back of a garage. He had come from an upscale family where money was never an issue and there was a TV in almost every room. Before long, James found himself dropping in on his parents, especially around dinnertime. They would invite him to stay and eat dinner. James would pretend that he was busy, but that he could manage to stay a little bit. Then he would play a few video games and before long it was bedtime, and he returned to his shack.

He reminded himself often that at least he was a free man. There was no one to tell him what to do, and no one expected anything from him. Then the inevitable happened—the first of the month bills were due. Rent needed to be paid and utilities were coming at him like snowballs heading downhill. He felt overwhelmed after he did the math. He did not have enough to pay his rent. The landlord gave him a short extension, but he wasn't sure that would be enough time. He made the round to his parents' home again, this time with a load of laundry. His dad asked, "How's the good life we have been hearing about?" Reluctantly James said, "I don't have enough to pay the bills. I didn't budget for food or gas or electricity." His dad asked, "What did you budget for?" James smiled and said, "Fun!" Then he concluded, "I have had more fun here at home than I have since I left."

This story fits any young man trying to find his own identity. This story is hypothetical, but all too often many young people want freedom without having the maturity to succeed.

In Luke 15 is the story of the prodigal son who was within his own rights to ask for his inheritance from his father. He didn't leave his father's house upset or angry, but he did leave unprepared. The inheritance carried him into a distant land where he found all kinds of fair-weather friends who loved to hang out with him. When the money dried up, all those who seemed to be fond of him and should have been there for him in time of need disappeared. Though he had left his father's house, his father never left him. He still carried the name of his father. He had not been disowned. He was just as wealthy now as he always was. However, his environment and circumstances did not match up with his position with his father. He was able to land a job slopping the hogs. His food was to share with the pigs.

Finally, the Bible says, *he came to his senses.* Really he came to the end of his plans and remembered what it was like living in his father's house. Perhaps his senses were the drawing of the Holy Spirit leading him back to the covenant he had enjoyed before he wanted to have a separate identity. In his father's house even the servants were better off than he was. The only difference was he was separated from his father. The only sensible thing to do was to return to the place where he could enjoy the covering of his father. The best part of this parable is that his father saw him a long way off and welcomed him home with open arms.

God is always looking for us to come to the place where we have learned to enjoy living under His covering and not to see it as a prison. In fact under the covenant covering of his father there was protection—as there is for us under God's covering.

Everyone was happy when the son returned, and the father ordered a party to celebrate. The contrast was the older brother who had stayed with the family business and was resentful of the father's acceptance of his wayward son. Though the elder brother was in the house, he had not learned to enjoy the love and benefits of his father. The prodigal son had lost the benefits because he stepped out from under the canopy of the father. Both sons had not understood how to delight in the joy of their father. The elder had the mindset of a hireling and did not realize he could have had a party any time he wanted because it was his wealth as well. One son was distant, the other blind.

The point I want to make here is there are those who serve in the church as hirelings and have not taken the time to enjoy the presence of God. We can spend our whole lives working for God and not enjoying His love and the position of simply being His child. The younger son thought he had so messed up that he was happy to be a hired hand for his father. The covenant never stopped for either son, but both did not know how to enjoy the benefits of their father's covenant covering.

It is possible to be in a group of believers and still feel like an orphan. There are those who carry His name but don't know Him as a Father who wants them to delight in Him. It is not your serving He is after, it is your heart and affection He desires. When there is no joy in your salvation and you are not enjoying special times of worship, ask the Holy Spirit to renew a child-like faith and joy in your heart and return to your first love encounter with Him.

> *Father in Heaven,*
>
> *I ask that You would lead anyone who is outside Your house back into a loving relationship with You. May those who have been hardened through religious ceremony and unfulfilled promises find the way to be restored under Your hand. I pray that You would restore unto us the joy of our salvation. I ask that expectation of every day would once again be part of our lives. I bless every covenant marriage that it would be exactly what You created it to be and that those who feel they are trapped inside a dead relationship would be able to have hope again. I call prodigal marriages back into a covenant covering to protect the relationship and the home.*
>
> *Thank You, Father, because You really do restore our souls.*
>
> *Amen!*

6

THE MESSENGER OF THE COVENANT

UNDERSTANDING COVENANT IS necessary to live in the prosperity and health God intended for us. It is like understanding the circulatory system of our bodies. If we don't understand that blood flowing through our veins and arteries is the difference between life and death, we may cut off that flow unintentionally with dire consequences. I may not understand everything about the circulatory system, but I know enough to realize that my eating habits affect the freedom or the obstruction of the life flow of blood throughout my body. Any part of the body that doesn't get sufficient blood supply dies. For instance, blood restriction to a leg could result in the leg being amputated to save the rest of the body.

In the same way, we can give attention to certain parts of living a covenant life and yet be obstructive to other parts. We can survive, but without the part that could have helped us live more productively. Let me be even more specific. Let's say a man is very considerate and loving and diligent in his service to God, but at home around his family he is sarcastic and belligerent. The part that is restricting greater joy and success is cut off. Ephesians 4:3 encourages us to be diligent to keep the unity of the Spirit in the bond of peace. Notice that the word Spirit is capitalized referring to the Holy Spirit. The Holy Spirit guides us into truth and is the executor of the estate of Christ; He will adjust areas where our spiritual blood flow is restricted so we can enjoy the full benefits of God's favor. The promise of Heaven is wonderful, but I don't want to wait until eternity to live in the full offer that Father God has provided.

TRIP TO DALLAS

A number of years ago Diane and I were making our monthly trip to Dallas to meet with pastors who were part of a network of churches with whom we had recently become associated. I was not looking forward to the two-hour drive and subsequent traffic jams. It was Monday morning early, and after ministering twice the day before, I was somewhat weary. We were about thirty miles out and thoughts began to flood my tired mind, *We don't know these people…they are probably only concerned about Dallas and not interested in us from East Texas.* I mentioned some of my thoughts to Diane; she listened quietly with only a look of "I have heard this before." Since I didn't get a nod of agreement to my miserable thinking, I offered one more point that was sure to get a response. Before I could finish my eloquent debate, she looked at me and said, "Turn around and go back home if your heart isn't in this, but mine is." She had the tone of the Spirit of Truth. "Well, we are this far, we might as well go ahead and finish the trip." Since I couldn't enlist her to join my side of complaining, I thought I might as well get it over with and move on.

We arrived a little late due to backed-up traffic, and Pastor Olen Griffing, whom I barely knew at the time, was just opening the meeting with about thirty pastors and their wives in attendance. To my surprise Pastor Olen said, "We are happy the Kirkwood's are here today, and I want Pastor Kerry to lay hands on us and impart what God has given him." I must have looked like I had gone into shock because he repeated the request. We found some seats and sat down. I thought to myself, *You don't want what I have right now.*

I looked over at my sweet wife who knew what I was thinking and she said, "I will make it easy for you, go ahead and ask." I said, "Please forgive me for being a complainer and resistant to the will of God this morning." She graciously agreed and then prayed a quick prayer for the anointing to flow through us. This group of pastors had been experiencing a refreshing from the Lord for quite some time, as well as we had been in my church. I quickly reminded the Lord that I had a promise from Him about the prophetic call, and I would be obedient to not hinder His work through me.

Diane and I circled the room laying hands on each of the leaders, and no one had to wonder if the Holy Spirit was present. We were the only ones left standing in the room and quietly left in awe of the Lord. I knew it was not about me but more about His covenant wanting to bless these servants. I left there with a huge lesson learned about the faithfulness of God and how complaining can restrict the flow of the Holy Spirit. Today I work closely with Pastor Olen as the director of that same network of churches called Antioch Oasis. I wonder if I had turned back that day and not made the trip if I would be doing what I am doing today.

Covenant with God personally and corporately has destiny connected to it. I wonder how many opportunities are missed because there was another spirit speaking to us. Since that time I have realized the restrictive force that complaining has in diverting destiny.

PLACE CALLED THERE

During a time of drought, due to the Word of the Lord through Elijah, God said to Elijah to go to the Brook Cherith and hide there, and He would command the ravens to provide for Elijah (see 1 Kings 17:4). Elijah's provision depended on following the instructions. The ravens were to go there, not over yonder or to another place of Elijah's choosing. Elijah didn't have a say in who or what would deliver dinner. After all, ravens are nasty scavenger birds. It was a miracle the birds didn't eat the food on the way to there. Complaining can interrupt the road to there. The experience with the ravens was only a temporary step to get Elijah to the place he was ultimately meant to be.

The brook dried up after a while; and in verse 9, Elijah is instructed to go to a widow in Zarephath who would provide for him. The interesting part is that God sent him to a lady who was on her last meal and preparing to die. The widow did not complain or rebuke him for the audacity of telling her to give him her last meal. Her obedience released the promise of God to the point that the flour and oil never ran out until it rained. Timing and place makes a difference; however, complaining derails us from being in the right time and place.

GATE OF RIGHT TIMING

In Acts 3:2, Peter and John were heading to the temple at about three in the afternoon to pray. This was after the Day of Pentecost and they were now filled with the Holy Spirit, who Jesus had said was the promise of the Father. Peter and John were used to seeing a particular lame man by the gate called Beautiful. Perhaps they had given alms to him in the past; but on this particular day, everything changed. It wasn't a coincidence that the lame man was at the Gate Beautiful; beautiful is translated *horaios,* as the gate of right timing or season. Peter told the lame man that he didn't have any silver or gold but what he had he would give to the man. They reached toward him and lifted him to his feet, and he walked and leaped and praised God (see Acts 3:6-8). The gate that had been the place of begging was now the right place at the right time. It was the promise of the Father, and Peter and John were in sync and in destiny when the suddenly arrived.

GATES OF HELL

There are other gates that are significant in Scripture as well. The gates of praise that Psalm 100 teaches shows that it is through praise that we can enter into the courts of God, and there we can do the business of prayer. It is not called the gates of complaining. In the wilderness the ground opened up and swallowed 3,000 people who had been complaining against God for their diet and treatment in the desert. However on the Day of Pentecost, 3,000 people came to Christ. The redemptive side of God is part of His covenant. Complaining killed 3,000, and blessing on the Day of Pentecost saved 3,000.

In Matthew 16:18-19 Jesus announces that He will build His church and the gates of hell *(hadace)* shall not overpower the church. Here He uses the plural form of gates. Hell that is eternal separation is only one gate and not gates, at least in my mind. The word for *hades* here simply means to not see or to block the light. I believe there are well-meaning friends and influences that will block the light and keep us from seeing God's intended best for us. A gate of hades could be complaining because it is an accusation toward God that He has not taken very good care of us. If you know people who are habitual faultfinders and complainers, they usually cannot see anything good in any situation or in others. They find it comforting to have an opinion about any and everything. In many cases it is masking loneliness and crying for attention to be loved by their father.

Jesus gives us the tools or keys to ensure there will not be attempts to block the light or revelation of His goodness to us. In Matthew 16:19, Jesus gives a promise to those in covenant with Him. We have to exercise the authority here on earth to tie up the attempts to obstruct our covenantal rights as citizens of the Kingdom of God. We also have the privilege to release those things that bring light and revelation just like it is in Heaven. Since it has already been bound in Heaven, you and I have the right to do it here on earth. Since the light is already loosed in Heaven, we can call into the now to any situation that is obstructing the will of God. Jesus showed us how to pray in Matthew 6. We can pray, *"Let Your will be done on earth as it is in Heaven."* We should have an expectation to break through gates of hades to release the gates of praise.

Kay sent me the following email after reading my book *The Power of Blessing*. The principle fits here as well because it positions us to enjoy the covenantal benefits of His Word.

> I met my friend one day so we could catch up with each other and have some prayer. I said, "I will pray first and if I forget to mention anything jump in after I finish." Well she did; when I had finished, my friend began praying and I couldn't help but notice how she was blessing everyone who she was having difficulty with. I was shocked and astonished because this is the first time I had ever heard prayer like this.
>
> I mentioned to her that the prayer for her co-workers was amazing and it takes a strong person to bless someone who harasses you the way they have. I don't remember if she commented, but I was thinking

about how powerful her blessings on her co-workers were. A week later, at my surprise, I received your book in the mail from a good friend in another state who knew nothing of my constant thoughts about my friend and her way of praying for those who are mean to her. I was hungry to know more about this type of praying.

I started reading your book earlier and read it nonstop until I finished it. A line that stood out to me was "cursing causes darkness to thrive, and blessing turns things for righteousness sake" (58). It's the truth and it sounds like poetry. It has changed my perspective of how I view difficult challenges. I have changed my language from being a complainer to one of blessing. I feel the "power of blessing" will make my marriage stronger.

If you are sitting at the wrong gate hoping luck will come your way, you will be sorely disappointed. The gate of complaining is a gate of hell that will hold you there and keep you from seeing the goodness of the Lord in the land of the living. Psalm 1:1 says, *"How blessed is the man who does not walk in the counsel of the wicked, nor stand in the path of sinners, nor sit in the seat of scoffers!"* Where you sit in life is how you will view everyone and yourself.

Ephesians 2:6 tells us that God has raised you up to sit with Him in heavenly places in Christ Jesus. If you are sitting among complainers or scoffers, you won't be able to see when the right gate comes your way. God has a place called "there" for you. Take your place and be seated in the heavenly places so you can see the things you should be binding and the things you need to be loosing. Change is coming your way as you are reconnected to the covenant promises He has purchased for you.

MESSAGE OF THE COVENANT

God is very serious about His covenant and the promises that are connected to the covenant. He says in Jeremiah 1:12, *"I am watching over My word to perform it."* Perform here is more than just doing it. It is derived from the concept *asah,* to make. In the broader sense of the word it describes a creative process much like one seed can produce a whole tree. This verse is more complete when we say He watches His word to see it reproduce to the full potential. Isaiah 55:11 similarly says, *"So shall My word be which goes forth from My mouth; it will not return to Me empty, without accomplishing what I desire, and without succeeding in the matter for which I sent it."*

There is life in the Word itself and its potential is to bring God's fullest intentions into being, and it won't stop until it is finished. God's Word and covenant is irrevocable. It is now a sent word that where and with whom it finds agreement it produces after its kind. Fear produces or performs after its kind or nature. Job said, "that which I feared came upon me." The opposite can also be true: that which I believe in faith will come upon me. It depends on what seed we have allowed to be planted inside us. Either one will produce and perform what it was sent to do.

PROVISION OF THE COVENANT

About fifteen years ago I was faced with having to contend for the report of the Lord over the report of people. My church had been experiencing such refreshing that many times people had to be driven home by others because they were overtaken by the sweet presence of the Lord. Some meetings it was apparent that Acts chapter 2 had been repeated because some people appeared to be inebriated. This refreshing lasted continually for about six years.

I felt prompted of the Lord that I was to share with the church a series of messages on covenant.

During that season there were families driving from neighboring towns to attend. There was misunderstanding as to my motives for sharing on covenant. They had heard the term used before and immediately interpreted it to fit what they had experienced in the past, which was not good. They had come from the shepherding movement where the idea of covenant was used to apply to honoring leadership. They had a bad taste in their mouths over the message of covenant. I was not even thinking along those lines at all. I was seeing covenant as God's Word over our lives. Nonetheless, some of them were the strongest givers and one said to me, "This church won't be able to survive without the giving of our group." I said in return, "No one owns a church; it belongs to God, and He will supply or this church should not be here."

I continued to sense the Lord saying to me, "Just be a messenger of the covenant." Our staff and elders committed to praying for the Lord to direct the way we should pray. We continued to pray for God to establish His covenant in the community. Before long the surplus funds we had dwindled to the point where we needed to do something. One evening in an elders' meeting I told the eldership that the Lord told me I was to lay down my salary and trust Him. They were gracious saying, "You can't do that, you are the founding pastor." I was grateful for their concern, but the Lord spoke directly to me and also said that none of the other staff would need to reduce their salaries. The verse the Lord gave me was that the father was to lay up for the children. I was the father of the house and the children of the house don't lay up for me. The next step was to explain this to Diane. When I told her, she smiled and said, "I got the same message from the Lord a few weeks ago, but I told the Lord He would need to speak to you."

In just a few weeks I received a call from a man in the church who owned an automotive shop and he sounded rather urgent when he said, "You need to come to the shop right away." I asked if everything was ok, and he assured me it was "very ok." I dropped what I was doing and headed to his shop. When I arrived, he explained that he had helped a widow lady from time to time doing minor things on her car. I wondered what that had to do with me and wanted him to get to the point. Then he pulled a check from his pocket and said the woman had come in today and said, "I felt like the Lord wanted me to give you this for your church." The strange thing was she didn't even know what church he attended. The check was for $15,000—exactly what we were behind for the year.

I never met the lady, and for the next five years she gave a check to the church through her mechanic. Some years she gave $30,000 and some years $20,000. The year that she no longer gave was the year we had a financial breakthrough, and the year I went off salary was the largest income Diane and I had ever had. The Lord brought sources from all over the country. I realized my salary was a ceiling that capped what God wanted to do. The salary was a limitation to us. Today the church enjoys a healthy giving spirit. Crisis can bring change, and preaching on covenant started the change we needed. God is faithful to watch over His Word to perform it and it is more than just meeting the need, He wants to cause the cup to overflow so we can be a blessing to all the families of the earth. I still want to be a messenger of the covenant.

If you are feeling abandoned by those you thought you could depend on and were disappointed, today the Lord wants to give you a message from His covenant. If others fail you, His word can bypass people and give you more than what you would have had before. He will out-perform your expectations. He wants to bless you to the level of His covenant and show that your dependence lies not on others but your trust is in the Lord.

REVELATION OF THE MESSENGER OF THE COVENANT

*"Behold, I am going to send **My messenger**, and he will **clear the way** before Me. And the Lord, whom you seek, will suddenly come to His temple; and the **messenger of the covenant**, in whom you delight, behold, He is coming,"* *says the Lord of hosts* (Malachi 3:1).

The job of the messenger was to clear the way before the Lord. Most scholars say this is likely referring to John the Baptist who was called to be a voice in the wilderness preparing the way of the Lord. Notice there is the messenger and then there is the messenger of the covenant. Others believe it is also Christ incarnate overseeing the covenant. I needed to understand what the messenger of the covenant was since I was using the term as a basis for what the Lord had impressed me to do. The messenger was not the focus, it was the message of the covenant. It wasn't about John the Baptist. In fact, John said, "I need to decrease, so that He (the Covenant One) may increase." This verse in Malachi calls for the "messenger of the covenant." In this verse the word for messenger is *arcaleos*, which is the same word for angel. In a way, we could also translate the "Messenger of God" as the "Angel of the Lord."

It is important to understand that when I reference the messenger of the covenant, it's not just the person who brings a message on covenant, but it is also the covenant message itself. My point here is the message about covenant is so important there was assigned a messenger to oversee covenant. The "angel of the Lord" oftentimes was a term referring to Christ incarnate before He came to earth as Jesus. The covenant message is not just another random sermon topic; it is the plan of God from the foundation of the earth, in which the Lamb of God would take away the sin of the world. The covenant was not Plan B. It was seen before the Fall of man because God knew that man could not keep the covenant. This lets me know the emphasis God has placed on this message, because He has assigned an angel to be in charge of preparing the way for the New Covenant.

CLEARING THE WAY

Malachi 3:1 opens with saying that the Lord will suddenly come to His temple. The word suddenly *(pehthah)* means to open the eyes as in a quick blink. He wants us to open our eyes to the truth of His covenant. One of the jobs of the messenger is to clear the way. In other words, every obstacle that hinders moving forward or causes a detour will be taken out of the way. The crooked places will be made straight (see Isa. 40), the low places brought up, and the high places brought down for a highway of holiness to come.

As we embrace the covenant message, we will notice a closer walk and less taste for the works of the flesh. The message of the covenant is not only about the return of Christ, it is also about our return toward Christ. The message of the covenant is a message about intimacy with the Christ of the covenant. The deeper this message gets inside, the more it will remove old baggage and letting go of unforgiveness and embracing His message of forgiveness. At the center of covenant is the revelation of forgiveness. Jesus used a story to show this importance in Matthew 18:22-35. The parable depicts two slaves who were brought into account for what they owed the king. One owed ten thousand talents, which is a huge amount of money. He begged for mercy so his family would not be put into debtors' prison. The king responded with mercy and forgave the huge debt. Then later the king heard about the same slave who was owed a few denarii, which was just a few cents, and he was demanding his fellow slave to pay or go to prison. The king was angry because the one who was forgiven did not forgive another servant, so he was put into prison for his unforgiving heart. The message is clear that most people want the benefits of covenant but not all pay it forward to others with the same mercy.

The covenant is all about forgiveness and is all about resisting the proud and arrogant who won't forgive. Forgiveness comes from a heart of giving. God so loved that He demonstrated this love by giving His only Son. Envy, jealousy, and bitterness are enemies of the covenant.

REMOVING STUMBLING BLOCKS

One of the phrases used in the New Testament is "stumbling block." It was a very common term used in biblical times. A stumbling block was a very cruel trick that was often used by the children and youth. When the kids saw someone who was blind or handicapped, they would toss a piece of wood or a rock in front of the person causing the person to stumble or fall. When the person fell, the bystanders would mock or laugh.

Stumbling blocks can be obstructions that cause people to fall or lose their balance or direction. So when Scripture talks about removing a stumbling block, it means removing those things that would interrupt or distract you from moving forward on a straight path. Stumbling blocks can be tangible things like a job, friends, relationships, and hobbies, or intangible like anger, unforgiveness, bitterness, sexual promiscuity, or other unconfessed sins.

When people have a covenant-breaking spirit, they will be quick to want to make a personal covenant; but the first time they don't get their way, they break covenant. If all it takes is an offense to make them end a relationship, then it means that they never really were in covenant—or at least don't understand it. Sometimes people take an opportunistic moment when a covenant is just a matter of convenience or comfort. For some the old adage applies, "I'm just going to hitch my ride to you until I can get a better deal." Selfishness is a covenant-breaking spirit and is responsible for the majority of divorces. I know many say their needs are not being met and have convinced themselves of what they are missing, but it boils down to the same spirit of selfishness. The message of the covenant is to deny yourself and take up your cross. The cross is not bondage, it is the way of liberty.

FRIENDS CAN BE STUMBLING BLOCKS

Jesus recognized stumbling blocks that were thrown His way. In Mark 8:33-34 Jesus explained to the disciples the things He had to suffer, the rejection, and ultimately His death. Peter took Jesus aside and rebuked Him, but Jesus interrupted him by saying, *"Get behind Me, Satan; for you are not setting your mind on God's interests."* Jesus said in the next verse, *"If anyone wishes to come after* [follow] *Me, he must deny himself...."* The word deny implies to take a lesser thought for yourself.

So Jesus recognized this stumbling block Peter was tossing, even though he had right before declared to Peter that he was a chip off the Rock, *petros*. Peter had rightly said that Jesus was the Christ, the Son of the living God. How could someone be so right one moment and the very next be so far off?

Peter's discernment was working great, but his character needed some maturity. Perhaps when Peter heard that the plan was for Jesus to die, his selfishness kicked in. He began to think, *What about me; I have given up my business and followed You. If You die, what will happen to us? As long as Jesus is with us we can draw the crowds. We always have food when Jesus was with us; we would just go fishing.* Peter was seeing Jesus from his selfish view and not from the view of Him being the Messenger of the Covenant and at the same time being the Covenant Sacrifice. Being a follower of Jesus was easier than being a leader after He is gone.

Fortunately Peter did learn what it meant to deny himself. He later denied Jesus three times, but when the power of the covenant got inside of him, it transformed him so much that Peter was one of the greatest apostles of the church. History books record that Peter, like Jesus, was crucified for his faith; but Peter thought he was not worthy to be crucified in the same manner as Jesus so he requested to be crucified upside down. It wasn't until Peter was cleansed of selfishness could he fulfill the purpose of God.

DON'T STOP SHORT OF THE PROMISE

If we don't understand directly how God moves and works in our lives, then we will get distracted easily. It is too easy to take a good thing and interpret it as a "God thing"; and we'll miss our destination. If we are not sure of our destiny, then any road will take us there. God really wants us to see where He is taking us. We may not know every detail, but we can at least know the direction. Proverbs 29:18 says, *"Where there is no vision, the people are unrestrained."* Another translation says, *"Where there is no on-going revelation, the people are scattered."* Romans 3:23 says, *"for all have sinned and fall short of the glory of God."* The New Covenant is certainly glorious with all the promises the Father has given to us through His Son. From these verses we can see that it is possible and many do come short of arriving at the fullness of God's intended blessing.

One of the sad history accounts of Abraham's father is in Genesis 11:31. Terah, Abraham's father, left the land of Ur of the Chaldeans for the purpose of going to Canaan. He took all of his family and traveled as far as Haran and settled there. The name Haran is translated as "parched," however Canaan is translated as "to bend the knee" or to worship. Terah had a destination in view but something happened to cause him to settle for parched instead of worship. He settled for parched while the promise was still ahead. We are not told directly as to why he came short of the destiny. Perhaps Terah was tired of the travel and became comfortable in Haran.

It's easy to get distracted with good things and miss the God things. Without keeping in vision where we are going, any place will seem like home. I am not just referring to a physical location but more closely to a spiritual condition. I am sure you have known some who begin with a vision and are very passionate for a while, until the vision is tested and passion alone cannot take them to the next level. Apostle Paul says everyone who runs the race runs to win, but only those who finish receive the prize (see 1 Cor. 9:24). The starters aren't the ones who are celebrated, only those who count the cost and refuse to stop until they get to their destination are celebrated.

Jesus had finishing anointing. He could have called off the whole thing. While in the garden of Gethsemane He prayed, *"if it is possible, let this cup* [covenant] *pass from Me; yet not as I will, but as You will."* Jesus chose not to stop short of the covenant. Though He felt the weight of the world and its sin upon Him, He chose to finish what the Father had sent Him to do. While on the cross, while being mocked, He could have called a legion of angels to set Him free from the hideous moment, but He remained nailed to finish the cup of the New Testament we call the New Covenant. When Jesus cried out with His last breath and said, "It is finished," the veil in the temple that separated the Ark of the Covenant from the people was torn from the top to the bottom. The tombs of old saints who had died under an Old Covenant were opened (see Matt. 27:52) and the saints came to life and entered the Holy City and were seen by many that day. If Jesus had stopped short of the glory of His destiny, we all would be slaves to sin today.

THE FIRE OF COVENANT

The last point I want to make concerning the Messenger of the Covenant is that He will be like a refiner's fire. A refiner, also called a smelter, would heat up metals to their purest form in order to remove any mixture, particularly with gold, that would lower its value. Part of the oversight of this messenger was to separate the worthless from the valuable. In order for us to allow the covenant to be more than just a doctrinal belief, it has to become part of us in an intimate way. At the point of refinement the covenant is no longer a contract on paper but becomes written upon our heart. It also ceases to be an "it" to becoming Jesus who is the Covenant. The fire is not just a short-lived zeal that comes with a new program. He is the object of our affection. It is no wonder the Holy Spirit is oftentimes called The Holy Ghost and Fire.

Dear Lord,

Thank You, Jesus, that Your death and resurrection has allowed us to enter into covenant and fellowship with You. Please forgive us for stopping short of Your fullness. Forgive us for letting distractions, detours, and disappointments settle for less than Your best. Forgive me for any attitudes, complaining, anger, frustration, or mental strongholds that have caused me to step out from Your covering of covenant. Help us to allow the messenger of Your covenant to cleanse and write upon our hearts. Give us this day finishing anointing to finish with more passion for You than when we began. Please restore our vision so we can see clearly again.

Amen!

7

COVENANT-
BREAKING SPIRIT

WE WANT A DIVORCE

TOM AND SUSAN would likely have been voted as the most popular couple in school. He was an award-winning jock and she was leading the band. They were married in a traditional church with all the trimmings of a beautiful wedding. Their vows were ceremonious in nature and both pledged their love and faithfulness till death they parted. Soon after, they both were busy working on their careers and each were involved with different friends who were primarily connected to their jobs. Tom worked weekends a lot and was scarcely seen in church. Susan stayed faithful attending church and understood that at this stage sacrifices had to be made to build income and plan for the future.

Their time spent as a couple became scarce each passing month. Susan was busy with the routine of her job and the subtlety of being apart became the norm. They were both excited when their first child was born. But if Tom was to see his daughter, Susan had to take her to his workplace, because he was always so busy. Susan adjusted her schedule to be more of a mom, but still maintained a job with childcare help from grandparents.

Ten years into the marriage, someone discovered Tom was committing adultery. The affair had been going full swing for over a year. When Susan confronted Tom, he admitted to the illicit relationship but was not sorry. Susan offered forgiveness with the desire to work through it. Tom quickly replied that he no longer loved Susan, that the other woman had more in common with him. Susan asked, "Are you willing for another man to raise your daughter?" He curtly answered, "I can live with that."

Brokenhearted, Susan turned to her heavenly Father for comfort and help. Tom turned to the other woman, whom he eventually divorced also. At the time of this writing, Tom is on his third relationship, this time no marriage just common law. He continues to have employment issues and severe health concerns. Susan eventually married, and is happily married to this day serving God fervently. The effects of the broken covenant on their child brought about bitterness toward her dad that continues today. The insecurity and lack of trust affected her for years and has carried over into her own marriage to this day.

The term covenant breaker is found in Romans 1:31. The King James Version of the Bible uses that description; other translations simply say untrustworthy. Broken bonds of trust are difficult to repair and only the forgiveness and healing of a Covenant-Making God can restore them. A covenant-breaking spirit can be passed down through generations. It will show up as a familiar spirit in families that have chronic divorces. It soon becomes acceptable because it sets itself up as the norm. In some families it's a joke about an uncle who has had five wives. Covenant breaking is not just about finding another partner, it's about having God in agreement with the union. Each time it becomes easier to break covenant, and not just marriage; the trust factor begins to diminish and eventually there is cheating in business, sports, and relationships. Find someone who is dishonest in small things, and you are looking at a person who is a potential covenant breaker.

COVERING OF COVENANT, CANOPY OF COVENANT

When a couple enters into a marriage covenant, they are inviting the Messenger of the Covenant to enter into the marriage as well. Remember, He will watch over His Word to perform it. Everyone has times of stress in their marriage; but remember, the Messenger of the Covenant is there to help resolve any and every problem. He will keep our hearts tender so that no problem is too big to solve. Some couples have testified they could feel a protective covering coming over them when they faced challenges together with their spouse.

God never intended for us to go it alone; we all need help in keeping our marriages strong. Covenant comes with grace that empowers us to fulfill our promise. In marriage you don't wake up every day saying, "Lord, help me to not have an affair." The God who keeps covenant and mercy will help protect you from covenant-breaking spirits. In First Corinthians, in response to moral conduct (sexuality practices), Paul says, *"Do you not know that your bodies are members of Christ?"* (1 Cor. 6:15).

MARRIAGE IS A COVENANT, NOT A LEASE

The marriage covenant is one of the most serious covenants that we can make. Kingdoms have been built, treaties signed, wars fought, and history changed by marriage contracts between kingdoms. In the 600s, some of the Christian kings in France and England strategically wed their daughters to pagan princes with the objective of spreading the Gospel while strengthening their borders.

In the natural world a contract is between two people of equal ability to perform that contract. When people buy a house or car, they have the ability to perform on the contract and make the payments to complete the purchase. Equal sides come together to perform that partnership. A marriage is a covenant. Unfortunately in our culture, some people treat marriage as if it was a lease that they can move in and out of without penalty. There is a big difference between a lease and a covenant. When we move into a position where we view marriage like it is an optional lease, it minimizes the other person and is a slap in the face to God. Likewise there are too many people who want to treat their covenant with God as if it is a lease option. This hardening of hearts indicates selfishness and spiritual immaturity instead of honest love of the Father.

WARNING TO REMEMBER COVENANT

We are in a time that is being overrun with a covenant-breaking spirit. Covenant breaking is rampant in our culture, church, marriages, country, politicians, and companies. In the last days there will be a "Great Falling Away." Perhaps this is a forerunning spirit to that time. We pray not, but everywhere I look, it is tragic to see that covenant breaking has become the expected. It wasn't too long ago that a man's word was as good as his handshake; it was his bond.

Unfortunately we are surrounded by a culture in which breaking covenant is the rule instead of the exception. We see examples of the breaking of covenant in the millions of marriages ending in divorce and the millions of children who are aborted mostly from unwed mothers. If sexuality is not brought under the umbrella and protection of covenantal marriage, we will continue to have abandoned children before they are even brought into the world. As a nation we have broken treaties with the First Nation's people, and created mistrust throughout the ethnic populations. It is important to remember that covenant is not about personal convenience; it is based upon people who have a standard of truth and who fear God.

Diane's been going to a county in East Texas for some time to do intercession for the people there. Poverty is high there, and per capita it has the largest number of couples living together outside of marriage. I don't know how they determine that, but it is listed on the county statistics. There are many who claim to confess Jesus as their Savior but have taken on the behaviors of the world and are living outside of covenant. It is no wonder that poverty is higher there even though it is located near the oil field industry of Texas.

In business we see companies breaking covenant with employees who are considered too old or make too much money or they are getting close to receiving their pension. Then there are the major financial institutions that in reckless disregard for consequences, in reaching for more profits, cause economic ripples resulting in bankruptcy for millions of people and loss of their homes. When trust is lost, then devastation and disillusionment creep in. When a nation is no longer trusted by other nations, we have the beginning of implosion. National patriotism is pushed aside for personal gain and mammon takes over; soon to follow is the mantra "every man for himself." The spirit of anarchy begins with a deep mistrust for authority, which serves only to justify the breaking of laws and self-preservation.

We can see at the base nature of all I just described is a covenant-breaking spirit that starts with cutting ties with the foundations God gave to this nation. Once we break from God's ways, then it's on to breaking from one another and on to national rebellion and hardness of soul.

But most dangerous of all of the covenant-breaking spirits is the one that causes believers to lose their faith, and their value system is lowered to fit the culture. When leaders in churches become part of these statistics and prominent leaders have affairs in the church, it is not surprising when the bystanders see this behavior and start to wonder if there are any absolutes left. When we lose trust in our pastors and church leaders, it is then easier to say I don't want anything to do with church again and the excuses of apathy only increase.

On a national level, some of our political leaders have attempted to rewrite the role of America with Israel. Rejecting our covenant with Israel and not supporting its ownership and occupancy rights to the land God promised Israel as His covenant people, places our country on a slippery slope. This is a very dangerous policy shift for the American politicians and people to take, especially when Scripture says that those who bless Israel will be blessed and those who curse Israel will be cursed. The security and prosperity of America is due to our support and love for Israel.

A covenant-breaking spirit attacks the inheritance and values of generations and steals what was sown in previous generations. A covenant-breaking spirit has to be repented of, and if at all possible restitution made. Jesus said in John 10:10 that the thief comes to kill, steal, and destroy, but He came that we may have life and have it more abundantly. Jesus is making a contrast between Himself and the enemy, who is after one thing—to steal. He is referring to the devil as the enemy. What would they have that the devil thought worth stealing? The answer is the seed. Remember when Jesus was born and Herod heard about the King of the Jews, he ordered all the male children two years and younger killed to get the seed of the Messiah (see Matt. 2:16). The Pharaoh of Egypt attempted to kill all the male Hebrew children. The devil believed God when He told him in the Garden of Eden the seed of the woman would bruise his head. The devil has been attempting to steal the seed from the generations that might raise up a deliverer and lead a national move of God. Jesus said He came to give us more abundant life. The Covenant Keeper gives life fully, and the devil wants to abort the seed that will bruise his head.

IT TAKES THE FEAR OF THE LORD TO KEEP WEALTH

If you have read any of the history of Old Testament kings, you will soon discover the roller coaster-type thread that runs through their generations. For instance a king will have peace and prosperity and then the next generation king gets comfortable with the wealth and leads the nation into idolatry. They are dealt with by God and they repent and return only to find the process repeated. God's way is simple: realize that the Lord has prospered you, you must honor God with your giving, and do not forget Him and turn to other things. In essence don't bite the hand that has fed you all these years.

Deuteronomy 8:10-18 says that when you come into the land He has given you and you are satisfied and built houses and when your herds multiply, don't forget the Lord your God for it is He who has given you the power to make wealth to confirm His Covenant. If you become proud and think it is your strength that gave you this wealth, the Lord will testify against you.

God's prosperity was upon them as a sign of His covenant. He knew that at times of peace and prosperity people turn away from the supernatural to follow earthly satisfactions that they can touch and control, such as inanimate objects and idols. The danger with prosperity is that if we don't understand how we received it, we won't have the wisdom to know to keep it. Matthew 6:21 says that where your treasure is, there is your heart. The heart will follow what we consider is our real treasure. Some folks strain at the notion of tithing. Tithing means a tenth, ten is the number of testing so it's easy to see the tithe as a simple test to locate the position of our heart.

I know that God wants to do exceedingly and abundantly beyond what we can even ask or think. However, if our heart is not ready for abundant wealth due to the obvious test that we are not gracious in tithing on a thousand dollars, then we should not be surprised when the prayer for ten thousand is not answered because of our stewardship. Covenant wealth depends upon fearing God and honoring Him with all that we have and living in humility realizing every good gift comes down from the Father of lights (see James 1:17).

Part of what the Messenger of the Covenant was sent to do was to break the curse off of the people. Malachi 3:9-10 says, "*You are cursed with a curse, for you are robbing Me, the whole nation of you! Bring the whole tithe into the storehouse so that there may be food in My house, and test Me now in this,' says the Lord of hosts, 'if I will not open for you the windows of heaven and pour out for you a blessing until it overflows.'*"

The Lord Himself is making the statement and the curse was upon the people because they had withheld giving the testing offering or tithe. Proverbs 26:2 gives insight into curses saying that a curse cannot come upon you without a cause. Just like a swallow looking for a place to land so a curse can't land on you unless there is a nest built.

If not honoring God with the tithe is building a landing strip for a curse to land, then it's our choice, not by some random curse someone would try to put on us. If the treasure of the heart is to love God through recognizing Him for supplying through giving, then we are ready to be blessed, which is the opposite of being cursed. By not giving, we are making a spiritual declaration that God did not have anything to do with our income, so He doesn't deserve the first portion. The act of giving the tithe is an act of worship and a declaration that we worship the Lord God and not mammon.

Here is God's exciting promise to the obedience of tithing, *"I will rebuke [push back] the devourer for you, so that it will not destroy the fruits of the ground; nor will your vine in the field cast its grapes,' says the Lord of hosts"* (Mal. 3:11).

I have heard the argument that tithing was only required under the law. This is not true; actually tithing started with Abraham, four hundred years before the law (see Gen. 14:20), and Jesus scolded the Pharisees that they were so specific about tithing—giving a tenth of their spices—that they were neglecting mercy and justice (see Matt. 23:23). Tithing is part of the New Covenant.

BOOK OF REMEMBRANCE

Those who feared the Lord spoke to one another [encouraging one another to be obedient] *and the Lord gave attention and heard it, and a book of remembrance was written before Him for those who fear the Lord and who esteem His name* (Malachi 3:16).

This is very interesting to me that there is a book in Heaven with my name in it because I believed Him and tithed. Malachi 3:17 promises us that when God prepares His possession we will be treated like sons who will be spared as a distinction between the righteous and the wicked. Those who honor the Lord and pass the test of tithing are promised open windows and protection from any wrath.

PROMISE AND COVENANT DIFFERENCES

A promise is different from a covenant. The promise is only as good as the one making it. A covenant reveals the one making the promise. In the case of the New Covenant, the covenant speaks more about Jesus and His love for us and the character of His nature. Then His promises are spelled out to us through many places of the Gospel and the apostles writing to the churches. Second Peter 1:3-4 says:

> *His divine power has granted to us everything pertaining to life and godliness, through the true knowledge of Him who called us by His own glory and excellence. For by these* **He has granted to us His precious and magnificent promises,** *so that by them you may become partakers of the divine nature, having escaped the corruption that is in the world by lust.*

Peter says we were granted promises. Granted means that it was part of inheritance. Something is only promised when someone has a right to claim the promise. In essence, promises are the details inside the covenant. The covenant is the big print, the promises are the smaller print. There are hidden promises so we will search them out. Proverbs 25:2 explains this: it is the glory of God to conceal a matter and it is the glory of kings to search out a matter. God is not hiding anything from us to be cruel but rather to raise our appetite to know all that He has set inside the covenant for us to enjoy. It is similar to someone who was a pauper and discovered a relative had died and left the pauper an inheritance. Because the pauper didn't have much of a relationship with deceased relative the pauper assumed the relative was also poor. By assuming the relative was poor, the pauper did not inquire about the inheritance and so did not enjoy a new, more abundant life; things never changed.

The Covenant that Jesus died for and left to us must not just be assumed but pursued. The mystery of the Kingdom of God is only a mystery to those who won't search out the promises made to them. I think one reason why more people are not pursuing their inheritance in Christ is because they only know surface things about Him they received secondhand, like He lived and died and now we wait to go to Heaven. If we really get to know Him, we will soon discover He has rewards for those who live in faith right now on planet Earth.

Romans 4:19-21 gives the account of Abraham when he received the promise that he would have a son:

> *Without becoming weak in faith he contemplated his own body, now as good as dead since he was about a hundred years old, and the deadness of Sarah's womb; yet, with respect to the **promise of God**, he did not waver in unbelief but grew strong in faith, giving glory to God, and being fully assured that what God had promised, He was able also to perform.*

Abraham having a son was a promise, it was not the covenant. The covenant was to do with the land of Canaan and the generations that would inhabit it. The promise of a son was personal to Abraham and to his future. When promises become personal and intimate, you know you have connected a present saying word *(Rhema)* to you that you can stand on in prayer and use as a weapon in spiritual warfare.

The devil attempts to give promises too, though usually through fear. I once prayed for a woman who was convinced of such a promise. The devil had promised her she would die from cancer should she continue to pursue the things of God. She was reminded of all the family members who died of cancer. The more she meditated the more she gave her faith to the devil to perform the death sentence. She had more faith for death than she did for anything promised through Christ. It was through deliverance from the lies that she could see any light of God. The first step was to show her God did not give this because He sent His Son to bring life not death. She had to see the promise of healing purchased through the bloody lashing given to Him on her behalf. She had to believe healing was the children's bread and to accept anything else would be rejecting the bread Jesus wanted to give her.

If you have believed any lie the devil has tried to pass off as coming from the Lord, it can be broken off of you right now. The truth of the Son and what He has promised will make you free. If the promise does not bring joy to your heart when you meditate on it, then it is not from the Lord. His promises are yes to life and no to death. I pray now for your freedom from the lies of the devil, and that your heart and mind would be renewed to consider all the good things He has purchased for you.

I think Paul, in Second Corinthians 1:20, says it all: *"For as many as may be the promises of God, in Him they are yes; therefore also through Him is our Amen to the glory of God through us."* Because the covenant is ratified by death and resurrection we can agree, say yes, with the strength and validity of His promises. The Amen means: so let it be or come to pass. If I don't know the promises He has made to me, how can I agree or say, "Let it be to me according to my faith"?

Maybe like you, I was raised with what was called a promise box that was always sitting on the coffee table in the living room. My mother would remind me before going to school, "Have you drawn a promise from the box?" I said to her one day, "This is like taking a fortune cookie." I should have realized what was coming next. She sat me down and explained the eternal Word of God that was breathed out by the Holy Spirit. She went on to say the promises were not words of man—they were my inheritance, but first I had to claim them. "Now," she said, "what would you like to claim today?"

She was actually training me to memorize Scripture. Her favorite verse was Psalm 119:11 from the King James Version, *"Thy word*

I have hid in my heart, that I might not sin against thee." The word promise *(epaggelia)* is to announce for the purpose of confirming one's right to something. It would be similar to one giving testimony to the intentions of someone's estate. The will, or covenant, is filed, but the details of the will have to be read by an attorney or judge to probate the will in some cases. The Holy Spirit will guide you into all truth. Jesus is the way and the truth and the life. The promises Christ has given you will always give you the Way, it will always be Truth and it will always be Life to you.

Choose today the promise you will stand on and see the goodness of God in the land of your living revealed.

> *Lord Jesus,*
>
> *I ask that everyone reading this chapter would be free from any influence of a covenant-breaking spirit. I pray that our eyes would be opened to the Covenant-Making Spirit through You. Let Your Holy Spirit bring to remembrance promises that perhaps were given many years previous and refresh them to our faith. I know You have not changed Your word, so the promise is still valid and alive today. Help us to have patience and faith so we would inherit Your precious promises. Forgive us when we have been slothful in giving of the tithe so we might pass the test and show we are ready to be trusted with more prosperity. Restore to all of us the joy of our covenant salvation. Give us discernment to know Your promises and reject the lies of the enemy. Give us this day our daily bread, the promises that will feed us throughout this week.*
>
> *Amen!*

8

ARMOR OF THE COVENANT

------◆------

ONE OF THE great faith builders is Israel finally entering the Promised Land. They had been hearing the testimonies about the land and all that Moses told them. Now after forty years they would get a second chance to possess their promise. Forty years prior their fathers had the opportunity to have already inhabited the land but resisted because what they saw outweighed their faith.

When the spies returned with the reports of this new land, they confirmed many of the things God said about the land. There were houses that were already built just waiting for them to move into. There were vineyards already planted waiting for them to harvest the grapes. The wells were dug so they didn't have to spend time digging—everything was just waiting for them to take possession. The only problem, God didn't tell them about the giants that they saw.

In Numbers 13:33, ten spies came back with a factual report, but God called it an evil report. They said when they saw the giants they became like grasshoppers in their own sight and so they were in their own sight. Though what they said was a fact, it was not truth. Truth is what God says even when it defies logic. They chose fact over truth. It is the truth that brings freedom not facts. Truth doesn't deny the problem, it just doesn't let the problem stop the promise of God from being fulfilled. Notice when they saw the giants through their eyes they compared the giants to themselves so they became what they felt. Proverbs says as a man thinks so he becomes. Because they were thinking like grasshoppers, the giants perceived them the same way.

That day those ten (remember ten is the number of testing) spies set a course for the rest of the nation that cost them forty years of unproductive life. The forty years was the time for the rebellious generation to die in the wilderness while the next generation would have their chance to possess the promises of God. There were two men who I would call covenant men—Joshua and Caleb. Both men went into Canaan and saw the same things as the other ten and came back with truth and fact. It was the truth that moved Caleb to say:

> If the Lord is pleased with us, then He will bring us into this land and give it to us—a land which flows with milk and honey. Only do not rebel against the Lord; and do not fear the people of the land, for they will be our prey. Their protection has been removed from them, and the Lord is with us; do not fear them (Numbers 14:8-9).

This is profound and key for us to understand living in the New Covenant today. Caleb believed God to the point that nothing could hinder God's promise to him not even the sight of huge warriors. Here is the key, if God is for you (because of His Covenant) then whoever is against you, their protection and covering has been removed. The only defense they have is the fear they can project on you. The covenant of God carries armor for those who dare to enter His promises.

Now, forty years later, the only two who survived the wilderness, you guessed it, were Joshua and Caleb. All the people who died in the wilderness were under covenant, but never entered into the promise. It should be noted here that just because we are in covenant with God doesn't automatically guarantee we will possess the promise. The promises of God are entered into by faith on our part. Fear of obstacles causes the weak of heart to put off stepping into their inheritance. Hope deferred makes the heart grow sick; the best way to defeat fear is to remember the covenant and compare the problem with the size of your revelation of God.

God repeats this same promise to Joshua as he starts the transition from wilderness vagabonds to a prosperous nation. Joshua 1:3-5 says that every place they placed their feet God has given it to them; no man will be able to stand before them all the days of their lives. God had to remind Joshua to keep the people focused, to be strong and courageous. It wasn't the strength of their muscles God was referring to, it was their faith and resolve not to turn back. The previous generation failed at this same point in the possession of the promise, but this time they are moved by the covenant not by the view of strange, unfamiliar territory. God won't fight for you while you are running in the opposite direction from the promise. We are defeated when turning our back to the enemy; but when we face them, they are defeated.

BULLIES BEWARE

My older brother Randy is a gentle man; not many things will upset him. When he was a strapping older teen, two things for sure would fire up his boiler: the first one was if someone said something against a family member, and the other was seeing someone bullied. He had a soft spot for the underdog, and he would quickly even the odds. Randy was in high school when I was in elementary. I had told Randy how an older kid was bullying me after school. When you are that young, everything seems threatening. Randy tried to show me how to confront the bully, but I was out-gunned. I told the bully that my brother would come and whip him if he didn't leave me alone. The bully said some choice words about my brother, and I was all too eager to tell Randy the sentiments of my nemesis.

Randy was now in the fight. He was now personally on board. Sure enough, the next day after school our mother asked Randy to pick me up after school. Because I knew Randy was coming, I was very bold toward the bully. The bully threatened, and I told him to bring his best stuff because I was ready. My plan did not include Randy being late. Since I already had called the older classman's bluff, there was nowhere to go. I sure wasn't going to run or I would continue to put up with the harassment. I made my move toward the kid who was a foot taller and twenty pounds heavier. About that time I heard Randy's car coming with its loud Hollywood mufflers. I knew I couldn't lose now, and when the boy saw the look in my eyes, he just turned and left. He did however get a good look at Randy, which didn't hurt anything either. That was the last time the bully came to that side of the school. My fear of this kid was empowering him and making me look like a wimp. I didn't become stronger all of a sudden, I simply realized I had someone on my side, and I couldn't lose. We were family and the covenant of family gave me the courage to face down my enemy.

A bully spirit is the intimidation people feel when they perceive they are overpowered. The devil likes to overpower with thoughts of defeat and humiliation and visions of being mocked. Today bullying is at an all-time high because the cowards hide behind text messaging or other social media. Bullies love to spread it beyond the person to others to get others to join in the sport of dehumanizing an individual to the point that death seems a better option. Bullying is a demonic spirit that attacks those most vulnerable. Bullies become wimps themselves when confronted; they feel empowered through causing others misery.

COVENANT SOLUTIONS

In Genesis 3:15, God tells the serpent in the Garden of Eden, *"I will put enmity between you and the woman, and between your seed and her seed; He* [Seed of the woman] *shall bruise you on the head and you shall bruise him on the heel."*

The word enmity literally means hot hatred. God placed a dividing point between the devil and all he would try to do and those who have covenant. Notice the seed is already named as He and it is capitalized because it refers to Jesus as being the Seed who would come from woman and have power over the headship of the devil.

Adam failed in taking dominion in the Garden of Eden, which also included taking dominion over the serpent, the devil, that was in the Garden too. The reason the devil hates you and me is because of the covenant God gave us and that separates us from the kingdom of darkness. Sometimes the bullying you feel is the enmity that the devil has for us—the hot hatred because He, Jesus, has already bruised the enemy's head and we have the same right to bruise him on earth cause he has already been bruised in Heaven. Just like I became bold when I heard my big brother coming, you can you hear the coming of the Lord. He is with you as you face the bullying of the devil.

The Bible calls Jesus our elder brother. Jesus, our elder brother, has already bruised and cut off the headship and rule of the devil over the covenant family of God. I believe we can have a hatred for cancer that will put enmity between us and cancer or any other disease. When I minister to those who are sick, I don't try to find out all the doctors' reports and the level of the sickness, I won't give any ground to the serpent that strikes fear in the covenant people with diseases. We can drive out sickness because the bloodline has been drawn and our Big Brother has crushed the enemy. We may get hit on the heel, but we have the advantage of going after his head.

COVENANT SEED

As mentioned previously, First Peter 1:23 says we were not born again with corruptible or perishable seed but with incorruptible seed that is through the living and abiding Word of God. Jesus was the seed of the woman whom God promised would bruise the devil's head; and because we were born again, we have new DNA from the seed of the resurrected Christ. We have been translated from the kingdom of darkness into the Kingdom of Light. We have changed addresses and have changed inheritance from the fallen nature of Adam to the resurrected nature of the Messenger of the Covenant, Jesus.

Romans 16:20 says that the God of peace will soon crush satan under your feet. Because we have come from incorruptible seed, God is now using our feet to do the crushing of the headship the devil had over the first Adam. We now are partakers of Christ's divine nature. If you sense the old person you used to be trying to take over your thoughts and say things the new you wouldn't say, just stop and renounce the old self and say, "I no longer am a participant in your nature, I am born again, and I am a new species."

Being the seed of Christ puts enmity between you and the world's value system. You can determine how deeply His seed has taken root in your life by comparing the things that God hates or has enmity with and how you feel about the same things. For instance, look at Proverbs 6:16-19 that lists seven things God hates and are abominations to Him: haughty eyes, a lying tongue, shedding innocent blood, a heart that devises wicked plans, feet that run rapidly to evil, a false witness, and one who spreads strife among brothers. If we really want to know Him intimately, we need to know what He likes and dislikes to the point of hating these things ourselves. Being entangled in these kinds of things blocks promises from coming to fruition. The seed that will crush the head of the enemy must be free from the things that God calls abominations to Him. The blood of Jesus in the New Covenant doesn't cover sin—it washes away and eradicates sin.

Second Corinthians 9:10 reminds us that it is God who gives seed to the sower. If we follow this thread through to personal application, we see we are of pure seed and new incorruptible lineage. Now we see that God gives us seed to sow. He doesn't give us corruptible seed to sow but it is the seed of His divine nature. The tongue in Scripture has been called the rudder, and the power of life and death is in the tongue. The tongue spreads the seed, and when we are blessing others, speaking life over one another, we are sowers of the seed that is the nature of Christ—and this seed will bruise the head of the devil.

On the contrary if I sow strife and the things God hates, I am releasing the seeds of the serpent and the principle of reaping is the same for sowing corruptible seed as well as good seed. There are some who are under the covenant of Christ but are sowing corruptible seed, and yet they wonder why they don't see favor though they claim the same promises as someone who is sowing seed of blessing and life. Their resistance to the devil is weak because they have agreed with the gates of hell. Amos 3:3 asks how two can walk together unless they are agreed. Agreement in this context means to say the same thing. If you are praying one way and sowing seed that is saying what hell says, you won't find agreement in

THE SECRET POWER OF COVENANT

Heaven although you are loosing in Heaven. Isaiah 59:3-5 describes this process likes this, *"...Your tongue mutters wickedness... they hatch adders' eggs and weave the spiders web; he who eats their eggs dies...."* Corrupt communication is like incubating snake eggs, or in this case devil eggs.

The power of life is in the tongue to bring the seed of life to crush the serpent, or the tongue has the power of death to hatch the devil's thoughts and ideas. One who hatches the adders' bidding has no power over the enemy. Jesus said in John 6:63, *"the words that I have spoken to you are spirit and are life."* Remember, you are a new creation; old things have died and you are a new model with the seed of life that destroys the work of the devil. Choose life with your words because they are the seeds that you will eat from in the future.

WEARING THE ARMOR OF THE COVENANT

Being covered by covenant has many applications, I will mention just two here. A covenant of marriage is protection. First, the covenant vows, when taken sincerely and honored, bring blessing from God. Inside a covenant of marriage, the marriage bed is sanctified—any other relationship of an intimate nature is unsanctified. The enemy likes to probe the defense lines that God sets up in our lives. A few years ago I had just finished helping to facilitate a restoration meeting at a church with former members who experienced tragic abuse in the congregation. There was a lady who was brought in to do some special music for the occasion. After the meeting we were taken to a hotel quite late. The host made the arrangements and dropped both of us at the lobby. The lady said to me while I was signing the registry, "If you had been a girl, we could have shared a room." It took me a moment to catch the coded message. Then I looked up and saw her smiling at me. I laughed, and using Texas vernacular I said, "That dog don't hunt. I will tell you what I'm going to do: I'm going to my room, lock the door, call my wife, and tell her how much I love her." I turned and never looked back for a second glance. I knew the devil was testing the protection of the marriage covenant. I am protected with the covenant I made with Diane with the witness of the Lord. I don't see my covenant with my wife as restrictive, rather it is constructive for my family and everyone I serve in ministry.

The second area of covenant covering is with spiritual attacks. Ephesians 6:10-12 says:

> *Finally, be strong in the Lord and in the strength* [power] *of His might.* **Put on the full armor** *of God, so that you will be able to stand firm against the schemes* [strategic plans] *of the devil. For our struggle is not against flesh and blood, but against the rulers, against the powers, against the world forces of this darkness, against the spiritual forces of wickedness in the heavenly places.*

This type of covenant covering is of a spiritual nature. Paul warns us of the attacks against the mind and the unseen areas of life. Spiritual schemes are woven together to interrupt the momentum you are making in God. We have a covenant with the Father that gives us the right to resist spiritual harassment that manifests through fear or physical attacks against our health. The solution He gives: put on the complete, full, whole armor of God.

There must be a tendency for believers not to put on the complete armor for Paul to instruct us specifically to wear the whole armor. Paul is using the Roman uniform of armor to explain to the Ephesians that they are in a war over the territory of their minds. Their enemy was not a flesh king, the enemy came from authorities that gained a foothold in that particular region. Likewise, I have sensed different spiritual powers in various regions as I travel across the country and in other countries. They have different control and use that leverage to afflict the people in that region. For instance, when Jesus was casting out demons from the man living among the tombs, they identified themselves as a legion. The demons pleaded not to be sent out of the country because their authority had gained strength there in that region.

I have seen poverty at a dehumanizing level because of the principalities that have over decades entrenched themselves to afflict the people. The demons hate the truth about covenant. There are families that have suffered with numerous premature deaths in a family. Many times it can be traced back to a time of covenant breaking. These demonic spirits know that if they can cause covenants to be broken, whether in a marriage or in a city or a nation, they will have cause to enter that family or region.

I want to give you a short list of things demons do to cause you to break covenant with God or others. This is just a sample, not a definitive list by any means.

1. They plant lies and suspicion and make you think it is God showing you the evil things about others.

2. They try to cause your passion for worship to become lukewarm.

3. They will attempt to create division among the Body of Christ and plant offenses to uproot you from your place.

4. They will sow false doctrine to offset the truth and bring confusion.

5. They will try to make you feel unwanted and as if no one loves you to impart an orphan spirit.

These are just a few examples to be aware of so you will not be deceived by these schemes. The picture of the armor for this spiritual battle may appear to be physical, but the application when applied is spiritual protection. The order Paul uses for the armor is the same order that a Roman soldier would use to dress himself. The order has significance (see Eph. 6:14-17). The first piece of armor is the *belt of truth*. All the other pieces of armor are tied to the belt, and without the belt of truth everything else would fall off. For instance, the sword is carried in a scabbard hanging from the belt. The breastplate is tied to the belt, and cannot be pulled off overhead. Jesus, the Author of the New Covenant is called the Truth (see John 14:6). The covenant armor foundation is truth. The scheme of the enemy is based upon lies. The second order of armor is the *breastplate of righteousness* that secures the heart. The issues of life flow from the heart. If righteous values are compromised, the armor is weakened and an entrance is found to breach the defense; that is why righteousness must be fastened to truth.

The next placement of armor is the *"Gospel of Peace" that covers the feet*. Gospel, meaning "Good News," is what we are to walk in. When the peace of God rules, we have firm footing and won't get tripped by being trapped with an offense. Next we are reminded to pick up faith, which is a *shield*. Faith is the action we take on what we believe. Faith is not passive; it takes a stand. Next is the *helmet*, which represents the covering of your head. Your headship is not your own; you have been redeemed and your headship is Christ. It is covenant that is covering every part of your life.

The last piece of covenant armor is the *sword*. The sword represents the Word of God. The sword is the only offensive weapon, which is enough. The Word is always the weapon the devil can't contend with. He will try to confuse by creating doubt like he did with Eve in the Garden by saying, "Did God really say...?" The Word of God is powerful, piercing even to the marrow; doubt weakens the sword in our mouths. Isaiah 49:25 says that God will contend with those who contend with you. When you are clothed with the armor of His covenant, it won't be you fighting alone—He will contend in the battle as well.

One type of spirit that will attempt to disrupt prophetic vision is the Jezebel spirit. The Jezebel spirit can operate in a family, church, or individual, and people are often unaware of it. It first gains the confidence and relationship with those in authority such as leaders in the church or the head of a household. A Jezebel spirit is not a woman who dresses up in bright colors and puts on lipstick. I wish it were that easy to recognize.

A Jezebel spirit has many characteristics; one is that this spirit will distract people away from present revelation and try to bring another vision, creating two visions or di-vision. If you remember the biblical story, Jezebel was leading another prophetic spirit while she was trying to kill the prophets of God. She was trying to establish her own school of the prophets. She hates the true word of God. Her spirit will try to control the government of a local church and will cast doubt among people on decisions made by an eldership. This spirit can work through either men or women.

If there is a spirit of Jezebel operating in the home or church, it blinds the on-going vision and halts the progress of growing (see 1 Kings 18:4). It will want to control the finances in order to direct the vision of the house. If there is a Jezebel spirit, it will always cause you to want to run from the call of God. Look at Elijah, even after he had experienced the most incredible experiences on Mount Carmel, the threat of Jezebel caused fear, and he ran for his life. Controlling the prophetic vision, the direction of people, and using threats are some of the symptoms that suggest you may be dealing with a spirit trying to subvert the covenant promise you have.

CASTING OUT JEZEBEL

In some cases the Jezebel spirit can manifest through illness. The Bible says that the Jezebel spirit can put you in a sick bed. There are consequences of tolerating a Jezebel spirit (see Rev. 2:20). I was lying in bed a few months ago with an infection and plugged-up ear. Also, Diane had something going on with her eye. And all of a sudden, it was about midnight, Diane said, "Get up!" I was just getting comfortable and ready to fall asleep, so I said, "What? Who? Where?" And she said, "I'm not going to tolerate Jezebel! We're not going to let her put us in a sick bed!"

I said, "Well, why do you get a revelation like that at midnight? Why can't we get it about nine or ten in the morning?" Diane is all about prophetic demonstration, so I had to get up out of bed. I'm half blurry-eyed and I'm standing there, you know, by the side of the bed. She starts quoting a Scripture about Jezebel, "We will not tolerate you...you will not put us in the sick bed. I sanctify this bed as a bed for sleep, as a holy ground." I responded, "Praise God. Amen." That was the last of continual disruption of unexpected sickness.

Jezebel is a spirit that likes to interrupt, disconnect, and distract us from the very thing that God gives—whether it's prophetic insight, worship, reading the Bible, sleep or physical wholeness, or whatever. When you begin to understand and discern that you are being distracted from the things that God has said over your life in covenant or what he has called you to do, then it could be a spirit like Jezebel.

Lord Jesus,

Today we place ourselves in Your hands for protection from the deception of the enemy. Let the belt of Truth be firmly fastened in our lives. Any areas where we have allowed a covenant-breaking spirit to invade our home or church, please reveal it so we might repent and cast it out. We pray that we would have an on-going revelation of who You are as the covenant covering in our family. I ask that the peace of God would rule in each person who reads this and You would capture their thoughts and give them the mind of Christ. Open our eyes to see clearly and free us from any offenses that would disrupt the progress the Holy Spirit is doing in us. I pray that we would never be used to be a stumbling block to anyone, but in all things we would reflect Your love and mercy at all times. Strengthen marriages and reaffirm the leadership of Christ being the Head in our homes.

In Jesus' name,

Amen!

9

EXTENDING BOUNDARIES THROUGH COVENANT

*Shout for joy, O barren one, you who have borne
no child; break forth into joyful shouting and cry
aloud, you who have not travailed...Enlarge
the place of your tent; stretch out the curtains of
your dwellings, spare not; lengthen your cords
and strengthen your pegs* (ISAIAH 54:1-2).

———◆———

I AM CHALLENGED BY these verses that are promises to Israel of their restoration and increase as a nation. We can take this personally as well. The prophet was instructing them to get ready for something that is not apparent at the moment. You feel barren, but the way out of the barrenness is to rejoice and worship as if you already were full of children or have answers to prayers. The demonstration of joy is repeated as a prophetic response of faith. It's not a matter of the circumstance but a matter of seeing the turn-around coming. In this case, the prophet instructs to them to enlarge their capacity, to take in all that God is ready to do for them. Some people are so locked into grief they can't see anything good coming their way. The tent represents their present capacity, and he is telling them to pull up the pegs and extend their tent boundary as to have vision for what is soon to break through. Joy is the prophetic expression that something is moving our way.

Happiness is a sense of well-being of the soul based upon what has happened. Joy is a sense of expectancy in our spirit based upon what is getting ready to appear. This chapter is about helping you to see where you will be, not where you are. God calls those things that are not as though they are so we will be prepared for their arrival. One of the biggest limitations to seeing the tent full is being enslaved to an old pattern. Let me explain. Psalm 126:1-2 says, *"When the Lord brought back the captive ones of Zion, we were like those who dream. Then our mouth was filled with laughter and our tongue with joyful shouting...."* As long as they were captive in Babylon, they had stopped dreaming or being visionary. All they knew was the pattern of being slaves. They had not made plans to do anything else but slavery. Enlarge your capacity to dream and your tongue will take on a new song of destiny. The best defense against an enemy of grief is joy. Joy is an attribute of the Lord; that is why we can say that the joy *of* (not *for*) the Lord is our strength (see Neh. 8:10). Break out laughing, rip the tent pegs out of the ground, and extend your dreams.

Diane had been teaching first grade for a number of years when we married. At that time she was making 60 percent of our income. The church we had planted was only two years old at that point. While I was away on a missions trip, she and the Lord had a long discussion about her role in the future of the church. She loved teaching the young ones and seeing them learn and write their names for the first time. Even today occasionally one of her former students will come up to her in a restaurant and thank her for being such a wonderful teacher.

The Holy Spirit was prompting Diane to leave her profession as a teacher and be a full-time Mom and pastor's wife. She was doing all of it before, but now there was an emphasis on her ministry role in the young church being planted. She was quite willing to be obedient to the Lord, however there were some logistical issues that needed some clarification. She said, "Let's see if I have this right, You want me to quit the job that is supplying 60 percent of my family's income and go into full time ministry, starting an intercessory prayer group to pray for the church and the nation without any salary?" The response was exact. She knew without any doubt this was what she was to do, and she needed to act quickly because the beginning of the new school year was approaching. She said to the Lord, "As for my house, we will serve You with all of our heart and raise our children in a godly environment and put You first in every part of our lives including first in our giving, if You, Lord, will promise me that we will lack for nothing and that our children would also prosper." She wrote the promise out as if it was a legal document quoting Isaiah 54 as her legal grounds for asking, and she signed it. She still has the paper where she wrote out her promise to the Lord and the reply she felt was God's agreement. Habakkuk 2:2 says to record the vision so those who read it may run.

When I returned home she showed me the promise she had made and asked if I was in agreement. I knew the Lord was leading us, and it wasn't presumption on our part. I can honestly say that we have kept the promise Diane made that day, and the Lord was not slack concerning His promise as well. We have prospered beyond what I thought was possible for us. I can honestly say there were times when we were tested in believing the promise given to Diane. But each time we would read the promise and say we are in covenant with God and His promises are Yes and Amen to them who believe. We learned the secret to covenant during those days and we continue see it played out daily in our lives and in our children. Recently my son Kevin commented that the prosperity of our children is due in part to the covenant we as parents have kept with God. Now our children are learning that they too must establish their homes in covenant with the Lord to continue the generations of favor and blessing.

GOD SAYS, "ASK ME"

I can tell you that in walking in fullness of covenant with God I have experienced the truth of being in covenant with God and searching out His promises. We see the promises of God like medicine. We simply ask the Holy Spirit to give us the Scripture verse that we can stand on for the particular issue we may be facing at the time. From time to time the Holy Spirit will prompt one of us to ask for a particular amount of increase. Once we have the figure we are believing for, we then tithe or give the offering based on what is to come. God is prophetic, He wants us to know what is laid up for us in the future. The devil wants to remind us of our past, and the Holy Spirit wants us to believe for our future. Jeremiah 29:11 promises us, *"I know the plans that I have for you,' declares the Lord, 'plans for welfare and not for calamity to give you a future and a hope.'"* For us, giving is prophetic because we can only give for the harvest ahead of us, not for what has happened in the past. Prophetic giving has insight on what to give and foresight as to what will come from it. This is not about randomly pulling out a ridiculous figure from thin air; one must hear what the Holy Spirit is saying in cooperation with your faith because there is action that must follow what you hear. The promise needs faith to complete the testimony.

Now I Know

In Genesis 22 God tested Abraham and told him to go and offer his only son Isaac as a sacrifice. Abraham makes the trip up the mountain with Isaac who was asking relevant questions about where the sacrifice would come from. Abraham placed the responsibility back on God by saying God would provide one. I find this fascinating that Abraham was focused more on obeying God than wondering about what Sarah would think when he came back without their son. How would he explain to everyone about his son? Abraham goes the distance all the way through the process and agony of seeing his terrified son tied to a makeshift altar. At the last possible moment Abraham hears God telling him not to do the child any harm. Here is the quote I want you to note: *"now I know that you fear God, since you have not withheld your son"* (Gen. 22:12).

If I were Abraham I would be thinking, *Just a minute here, You are God and You already know everything from the beginning to the end, could You not have just said, "Hey, I already know your heart and the outcome is that you will obey," and save the drama and the terror?* One of the lessons here was for Abraham to know himself. He needed to know that his own heart was so committed to God that nothing could come between them. Abraham needed to see that God's promise to him could never become greater than the relationship the two of them had. The test needed to show the gift is not more important than the one giving the gift.

The question: had Isaac replaced the love and communion Abraham and God enjoyed? The question was answered that day. After the passing of the test, God increased the promise (in verses 17-18) that Abraham's seed would greatly be multiplied and they would possess the gate of their enemy and through his seed all the nations of the earth will be blessed.

With the passing of each test comes an increase of promises. Don't despise the test because it is filled with promises yet to come. Hebrews 10:35 encourages us not to throw away our confidence, which has a great reward. Inside the gates of covenant there are promises for everything that pertains to life and godliness. The covenant God had with Abraham was to extend to all the nations; however, the nations that hate Israel today are the nations that serve another God. The God of Abraham, Isaac, and Jacob will cover the nations that support and stand with Israel because of this covenant.

In Genesis 17:18-21, Abraham asks that Ishmael, who was fathered by Abraham but not by God, would live before Him. God said no, but because of His blessing on Abraham, He would bless Ishmael, but His covenant would be with Isaac (see Gen. 17:20-21). Ishmael was the son of the flesh, but Isaac was the son of promise. We need to make a distinction between blessing and covenant. Ishmael is blessed today with oil-rich land and has become large nations. The blessing is a temporary condition. Covenant is stronger than blessing and covenant cannot be altered; it is irrevocable. Blessing can be squandered and lost. It can be lost in one generation. However inside of covenant there is blessing that is sanctified and holy when presented to God as belonging to Him.

According to Romans 11, the rejection by the Jews has impacted you and me as Gentiles (foreigners) to enter into covenant that Abraham had with God. But make no mistake about it, the time will come (see verse 25) that the fullness of the Gentiles will be complete, and thus all Israel will be saved as it is written, *"the Deliverer will come from Zion, He will remove the ungodliness from Jacob. This is My covenant with them."* Verse 29 continues to say that the gifts and calling of God are irrevocable. If you believe that the church has somehow altered this covenant and replaced Israel as

God's covenant call, then you are missing the point of this book on covenant. We are blessed because of Israel not in spite of them.

The New Covenant that we enjoy today does not take away from what God will do with Israel. Ephesians 2:13-14 says:

> *He Himself is our peace, who made both groups into one and broke down the barrier of the dividing wall, by abolishing in His flesh the enmity, which is the Law of commandments contained in ordinances, so that in Himself He might make the two into one new man, thus establishing peace, and might reconcile them both in one body....*

Jew and Gentile becoming one in Christ. Even now there are Jews coming to faith all around the world. His covenant will be complete, and those who appear to be blessed now, blessing won't take them into eternity with a Holy God who keeps covenant and mercy. Jesus said in John 10:16, *"I have other sheep, which are not of this fold; I must bring them also, and they will hear My voice; and they will become one flock with one shepherd."* It is clear that Israel is the other flock and there will be the joining like Romans 11 details; there will be one shepherd, Jesus, and we will become not two bridal companies but one bride married to one Christ Jesus. He came as the Lamb of God that takes away the sin of the world (see Isa. 53), and He will return not as the lamb slain but as the Lion of the Tribe of Judah showing that He is the warrior King.

The Gentiles see Him as the Lamb of God, and Israel will get to see Him as the Lion of Judah (see Rev. 5:5). I realize there are many Jews coming to faith now and will not have to wait till His return as the Lion of Judah, the root of David. We also read the lion and the lamb will lie down together in Heaven. These two symbolic animals have two completely different natures but the two natures will be brought together as one new man in Christ.

There will not be two separate covenants to bring Jew and Gentile together as one. There will be the one New Covenant that will last for eternity—no longer separated by an Old and New Covenant but all brought under one Shepherd with one New Covenant purchased by the blood of Messiah Jesus.

COVENANT WEALTH CAPACITY

Deuteronomy 8:18 was part of the sign that God used to prove to Israel of the covenant He swore to their fathers. God said He is "giving you power to make wealth." The word power in many contexts in Scripture refers to either *dunamis* meaning force, or *exousia* meaning authority. However in Deuteronomy 8 it has a different meaning; it is the word *kowac* meaning capacity. The verse would read, "I am giving you the capacity to make wealth." Capacity has boundaries in which the person receiving sets the boundaries or capacity based on ability. For instance, Jesus used the parable of the talents to explain capacity. One person had the capacity for one, another had the capacity for three, and another for five talents. The determination for the capacity was evidently their trust-ability factor. This is the factor that takes into consideration past experience with, in this case, a talent or money.

The guy who had the least lost what he had. He saw the opportunity not to gain but to only maintain what was given him, in a protectionist manner. He wasn't thinking about what could be gained through investing what had been given him. His fear of losing cost him the opportunity of increase, and he lost the future trust in which his trust-ability factor was set. The other two recipients invested what was given them and were rewarded for their faith. The guy who had the five talents and had gained five more through investing it received the one talent that the maintainer had. It doesn't sound fair in entitlement cultures, but we have to realize that God is not fair—rather, He is just in all of His ways. None of us would entrust our savings to someone who has a history of burying the potential that we had envisioned for increase.

In the same way, God gives to everyone a measure *(metron)* of faith. Faith set can be measured. The Bible says there is little faith, there is no faith or doubt, and there is great faith. So if faith is a measurement for capacity, then I need to know how to increase my capacity, which I have a right to enlarge inside His covenant. Not every person will have the same capacity and not every person functions in the same level of faith. My father-in-law had wisdom in handling money. He has made several fortunes using this God-given capacity. He said, "Don't let money handle you; you must always be smart in handling it." His other observation was that, "Money will take over your life if you are not prepared for success." Financial success can be very deceptive and prideful. Some of the tests we will go through is for the purpose of testing our capacity and readiness to handle bigger assets and influence.

My friend, Bob, sought me out for prayer one morning after church. I knew Bob was increasing his capacity and had some recent raises on his job, so I was somewhat perplexed when he shared his request for prayer. He said, "I never had trouble tithing until I got into this new position." He said. "Before when I made five hundred dollars per week, I would put fifty dollars in for tithe because it belonged to the Lord. But now I am making twice that amount and I am struggling putting one hundred dollars per week in for my tithe." He said one hundred dollars is a lot of money "just to give away."

I said, "Bob, I can understand your dilemma and difficulty, and I can help you." He said, "Oh good, I'm glad you can help." I took Bob's hand and said, "Repeat this prayer with me." He nodded his head in agreement. Here is the prayer: "Lord Jesus, thank You for blessing me, but I am not ready to a handle a thousand dollars a week, so would You please reduce me back to my comfort of five hundred a week." I could not even finish the prayer before Bob dropped my hand and interrupted saying, "No, don't pray like that." He laughed a little and said, "I get your point."

If you want to grow your capacity, you have to be willing to gain a generous heart. There is a difference between ownership and stewardship. Ownership means that you have sole right to everything you have acquired. Stewardship *(oikonomos)* means to oversee the wealth of another. Joseph was the steward of all of Egypt. If you see that God actually owns everything, then you are a steward. You get to oversee what belongs to God, which is beyond anything you could acquire with your own ability. If Bob had understood he was a steward and was simply investing what God had given him, he would not have had so much struggle in tithing. When we understand stewardship, we better understand the part of the covenant that has to do with confirming His name as owner on everything. I am just happy that I get to be a distributor of His wealth according to my capacity. Another famous line my father-in-law would say, "Everybody can work for money, but fewer still know how to make it work for them." Anyone can be a consumer but not everyone will be a distributor of God's wealth.

Israel was not ready to take the land until they first knew how to keep the land they would inherit. Like the prodigal who wasn't ready for his inheritance, it took him away from his father and he squandered it on loose living and buying friends. The inheritance God was giving to Israel was to serve the purpose of security and a place to daily worship the Lord.

READY OR NOT, HERE WE COME

Now when Pharaoh had let the people go, God did not lead them by the way of the land of the Philistines, even though it was near; for God said, "The people might change their minds when they see war, and return to Egypt" (Exodus 13:17).

Though there was a shorter way to the Promised Land, the people were not ready for the land. It was theirs through covenant, but they were not ready to keep their new inheritance. They had never had to contend for anything before. The point I need to make is that the reason some have not received the promised inheritance is due to not having the capacity to hold what has been given. Don't be weary waiting; ask the Holy Spirit to guide you into the process of growing your capacity. God doesn't intend on wasting His inheritance. Remember when Jesus blessed the five loaves and three fish. All the people were fed, and the disciples were to gather the leftovers which were the baskets given to them, the distributors. The leftovers didn't fall on the ground.

Here is the rest of the story about inheriting the land. Judges 2:21-22 says that God will no longer drive out the nations which Joshua left when he died. So the Lord allowed those nations to remain, not driving them out quickly—*in order that the generations of the sons of Israel might be taught war, those who had not experienced it formerly* (see Judg. 3:2). This is fascinating how God set strategy in place for their inheritance to be secure from generation to the next generation. There been times in their history that they have lost their land and were scattered abroad for going into idolatry and turning their backs on God. They are now in their land and on a daily basis being threatened by war. God will not allow that land to ever be taken from them again. The nations that want to take the land do not realize that it was given by covenant, not by war. It is through God they possess the land and will keep it. When we support Israel we are agreeing with God's covenant.

I pray right now you are being prepared for your promise. I ask that your capacity will not shrink but you will be enlarged for such a time that is to come for you. He watches over His word to perform it in you. The test is yielding strength to hold your ground.

"INCREASE OUR FAITH"

Jesus was teaching His disciples concerning forgiveness and warning them it was inevitable that offenses will come; in the context of releasing forgiveness, they asked Him to increase their faith (see Luke 17:5). I wonder if they thought Jesus would pray a prayer and simply impart faith to them. Instead, He gives them, and us, two very specific ways for faith to grow. We have already learned that everyone is given a measure of faith to begin with. Jesus gives them first the analogy of a mustard seed. It is the smallest of all seeds, but when it is planted it has the potential of being large enough for birds to come and nest it the branches (see Luke 13:19). So lesson one is until faith is sown it is not growing, and you can't always tell by looking what the potential is until it is sown. James 2:26 says that faith without works is like a body without a spirit.

Second, Jesus gave to His disciples the parable of the servant who has worked in the field and when he has come in would you tell him to sit down at the table and be served? No, instead you would tell him "prepare something for me to eat and properly clothe yourself and serve me until I am finished eating and afterward you can eat." Jesus points out that you don't thank the slave for doing what is commanded because he has only done what was required (see Luke 17:7-10). So the second lesson for increasing your faith is to go beyond what is required. If you only do the minimum, you have not grown beyond the measure of faith you started with. The opposite is true; when you exceed the minimal, you move into increase.

The tithe is the minimal measure of faith. Ephesians 3:20 speaks to this by saying, *"To Him who is able to do far more abundantly beyond all that we ask or think, according to the power that works within us."* The power that is in us comes from being in covenant with Him who is the enabling one. He wants to exceed beyond what we think. If our thinking limits us to the average mediocre life of doing the minimal to get by, then we limit the excessive ability that can work through us. A lazy believer doing only the minimal time to pray and will only attend worship services on special occasions will find his or her capacity thimble size and won't hold much. Learn to be excessive and extravagant in your worship to the Lord. Just singing the songs is the minimal. Let Him know you love Him beyond the words that someone else has written in the song. Personalize worship coming from your heart. Be exceeding and be abundant in expression toward Him so the power of His Covenant is increased through faith. First Peter 1:7 encourages us to make full proof of our faith. We are in charge of setting the standard that will be used to measure our capacity.

———◆———

The first time I prophesied as a nineteen-year-old, my faith was stretched to the limit. The church was geared toward prophecy being heralded from the congregation. One Sunday morning I was so touched by the worship time I felt the prompting of the Holy Spirit to prophesy. When I started thinking I could be missing the timing and flow of the service and the possibility of being wrong in what came out of my mouth, I completely froze up. I went home feeling like I had struck out in the 9th inning with bases loaded; I let the team down. I know that sounds a bit dramatic, but at the time it was traumatic. I went to my room, lay across the bed, and asked the Lord to forgive me for letting fear of people get to me. I found comfort in promising that if the Holy Spirit ever decided to give me another try at batting, I would come through.

Little did I think I would be up to bat so soon! Next Sunday the unction of the Spirit was rising up inside me again, and I knew this time I would not leave dejected as before. I remembered somewhere there was verse that said something about "open your mouth and I will fill it." So I went with that and by faith I opened my mouth not preplanning what I was going to say; what came out was "God is good!" The astonishing thing to me was there was not another word to follow. Now I felt embarrassed because in my mind I saw it playing out much differently. I thought surely there would come some sort of revelation that no one had ever heard before that would astound everyone in the room. Instead they thought, *How cute, the young man stretched his wings a bit.*

Feeling somewhat confused, I made it to my bed again and proceeded to repent for missing the mark. This time instead of striking out I hit a pop-up that didn't make it out to the pitcher. To my amazement, before I had the chance to give a pitiful plea, I heard the sweet voice inside my heart say, "Am I not good, and is it not in my word?" I answered, "Well, yes, but it wasn't very deep." He said back to me, "I gave you just enough to see what you would do with what you were given. Obedience is not just opening your mouth but also knowing when to shut it." The latter I find to be a lesson still in progress for me.

Faith has a starting place for everything you will ever do. Decide when you will start and if you need to start over—that's ok too. The main thing is, don't stop increasing your faith. Enlarging your capacity is putting stakes out to mark territory that you want to extend toward. You might have aspirations to be a successful business person. Find a starting point by working for someone who can mentor you. Be the best employee they ever had, volunteer for jobs that may be beyond your skill level. Stretch your boundaries;

you will grow into them. You don't grow by taking the easy way out. Trust in the Lord with all your heart and don't lean to your own understanding.

Lord,

I ask that faith would be released in the readers right now and give us vision to extend beyond what we ever thought we could accomplish. The education that some gave up on because it seemed too hard; revive that in their hearts again. Restore dreams of success and actions that will start a new beginning. Cause the fear and defeat of the past not to be part of our future. We want to sing a new song—one of victory.

Show each of us the place where we have become complacent so we can start stretching our faith limits for breakthrough. Increase our faith, Lord, by putting another crease in our in-crease because I know there are more creases to come to the point we have no more room to contain them.

Thank you, Jesus.

Amen!

1 0

SECURING BOUNDARIES
THROUGH COVENANT

———◆———

T HE REPORT ON the local news said that the conditions for a tornado were favorable. We lived in what people called "Tornado
Alley." As the evening progressed and although it was still light
outside, the early warning sirens started blaring. It was the most
eerie sound I had ever heard as a twelve-year-old boy. I went to
the front door to look out while the screams of the siren sounded.
There it was—it was just a few blocks away. The sight was frighten-
ing. My dad was telling us all to get away from the windows and
get into the hallway.

My mother seemed to take on a different personality all of a
sudden. She stepped out onto the porch, by now we could see the
dust and debris swirling in the air. My dad called her name and
pleaded with her to get back inside. She didn't budge. I could hear
her from around the corner in the hallway. She said with the voice
of a general, "You destructive demon, you have no place to set your
foot on this property or harm any of my family. I plead the blood
of the Lord Jesus. Now leave this place and never come back!"

The tornado lifted before it got to our block and landed again in a vacant field half a mile from our home. I knew from that time on that she not only believed in the protection of being in covenant with Jesus, she lived under it. I don't remember a tornado ever getting that close again.

It is one thing to increase our boundaries, it is quite another to secure them. Covenant becomes a spiritual defense that keeps those who honor His covenant safe in their inheritance. We might want to even call them spiritual laws. When the natural laws of gravity are respected and believed, we don't fall from buildings or jump out of airplanes without a parachute. There are laws that protect us. For example, the covenant law of tithing—when the tenth is given, the other 90 percent is protected and the tithe was called holy. God showed His covenant of protection when the Hebrews left Egypt and entered into the desert. He provided a covering of fire at night to keep them protected from the harsh desert elements. He provided another sign of His covenant—a cloud by day to protect them from the scorching heat. Every day when they gathered the manna, they were witnessing covenant. Covenant was all around them and yet they took for granted the miracle of covenant. Learning how to secure what the Lord has blessed us with is as important as knowing how to receive His promises.

> *A highway will be there, a **roadway**, and it will be called the **Highway of Holiness**. The unclean will not travel on it, but it will be for him who walks that way, and fools will not wander on it. No lion will be there, nor will any vicious beast go up on it; these will not be found there. But the redeemed will walk there, and the ransomed of the Lord will return and come with joyful shouting to Zion...* (Isaiah 35:8-10).

Here is the promise with some conditions for a safe place to share the blessings of the Lord. Isaiah calls it a roadway, allowing you to see that wherever you go you can be under this promise. This promise will take you into greater things of glory. This place is called a highway of holiness. Holiness is the condition to hold secure this ground. The Bible is clear when it says that without holiness no one shall be able to see God. When Moses saw the bush burning, God said to him from the fire to remove his sandals because the ground he was on was holy ground (see Exod. 3:4-5). Was the ground always holy at that site; when did it become holy? The ground went from being common to holy when God showed up. Moses could no longer just walk around as he had before, since now the ground was holy.

One reason why we see friends and family lose ground they had claimed is due to not realizing when the ground is holy—we have to walk there in holiness. The devil cannot defeat us on holy ground. It is only when we contaminate the place by allowing unclean practices to live and function on our highway. Moses first had to recognize the bush was not just a common everyday bush. Yesterday it was a common bush, but today it is holy and it will never be ordinary again. When we fail to see the deity of God on what He has permitted us to oversee, we will slack off in guarding the holiness of who we are.

Because of covenant we are called a holy people (see 1 Peter 2:9), a holy nation, a people for His own possession that we might proclaim the excellencies of Him who has called us out of darkness. God calls us holy because we are His ground. In His covenant we become His property. Paul said that our bodies are the temple of God and He makes the temple holy because of the cost He paid for a holy people. In Acts 10, Peter was having an open vision of animals he considered not clean; a voice from Heaven urged him to eat. Each time, Peter, sticking with his tradition, said by no means

THE SECRET POWER OF COVENANT

would he ever eat anything unclean. His religious traditions had caused prejudice between Jew and Gentile. Finally the voice from Heaven tells Peter, "What God has cleansed, no longer consider unholy" (see Acts 10:9-16).

Peter then goes to Cornelius' house; he was a Gentile. The Holy Spirit came upon Cornelius, and Peter was amazed that a Gentile who was considered unholy had received the Holy Spirit. The blockage for Peter was his prejudice and what he considered to be holy ground. When the covenant is embraced, it takes in new territory and the new ground is then holy. In order to secure the territory you have claimed and extend your boundaries, you have to walk in holiness. Holiness gained it and holiness will keep it sanctified (set apart for exclusive use).

Holy doesn't mean faultless or an outward look of what some call holiness. It is a work *(hagios),* which means exclusive of something. Second Timothy 2:20-21 really makes this definition clear:

> *Now in a large house there are not only gold and silver vessels, but also vessels of wood and of earthenware, and some to honor and some to dishonor. Therefore, if anyone cleanses himself from these things, he will be a vessel for honor, sanctified, useful to the Master, prepared for every good work.*

Paul was describing a typical Middle Eastern home at the time. There were vessels that served different purposes. A vessel of honor was a vessel that was holy because it was only used for one exclusive use. For instance there were vessels used to dig in the ground and after it was washed people could eat from it. There were pots that were used for toilet purposes, which were called vessels of dishonor. However there was one vessel that they would drink from that was not used for anything else. It was deemed *hagios* or holy because it was exclusive. Paul is calling us to be an exclusive vessel that is used only to honor the Lord. A covenant is exclusive to those who will keep the highway of holiness free from things that do not belong to an exclusive covenant.

Holiness is not about an exclusive look but an exclusive heart. Jesus told the Pharisees that they had cleansed the outside of the cup but left the inside dirty. I would say the cup Jesus was talking about was how they wanted to appear to people publicly but privately the cup was not exclusive or holy; it had been for both clean and unclean uses. So by definition we would have to conclude the Pharisee cup was not a cup of honor.

In Ephesians 4:27, Paul says do not give any ground to the devil. Ground also is translated as opportunity. Set boundaries in your life and family that will seal up any broken areas that would give an opportunity to the devil. Any unforgiveness is an opportunity for the enemy to gain a foothold. Matthew 12:29 states that no one can enter a strong man's house and carry off his property unless the person first binds the strong man. Then he can plunder his house. The only way we can lose ground or property or family is for the head of that household to be bound.

We have learned that a life given to the Lord exclusively, allowing Him to have preeminence, will secure the ground because it is holy. Therefore, we need to be aware that when the gatekeepers of the family or the heads of a business open the door to unholy practices, they are then bound and tied. When bound up, our precious family or employees are affected by the breach. A broken marriage vow causes children to be uncovered, and many times they are found by the enemy and they feed into anger and the same deceitful practices that opened the gate to begin with. There are no secret sins that won't eventually manifest in those we are sworn to protect.

THE SWORD WILL NOT LEAVE YOUR HOUSE

It says in Second Samuel 11:1-2 that in the springtime when kings go out battle, David sent Joab, and David stayed in Jerusalem. At the time when kings would go out and secure their boundaries and replenish their spoils through conquest, David did not go and do what normally he would have done. Many know what follows in this story. David was not focused on keeping his boundaries secure; he was lax and apathetic and his eyes wandered from his rooftop and saw Bathsheba bathing. He was struck by her beauty and it didn't matter what he had to do, he wanted her. However, she was the wife of a faithful soldier, Uriah. David arranged for Uriah to be killed in battle. When leaders use their authority to destroy others, there is a breach of covenant and their own boundaries have been broken through. Nathan the prophet delivered a scathing word from God to David saying, that because you have despised the word of the Lord by doing evil, since you have killed Uriah by the sword and have taken Uriah's wife, the sword shall not depart from your house because you have despised God (see 2 Sam. 12:9-10).

David was the gatekeeper for his house and he had opened the gates and his secure boundaries were weakened because of his own lust and covetousness.

When you read the next couple of chapters, you can plainly see that David brought defeat to his own family. Not only was it the sin of murder and adultery, but also it broke the boundary of holiness that had kept them safe for so long. The sword is turned on David when his son Amnon rapes his sister, and David's other son, Absalom, sets up Amnon to be murdered to avenge his sister. Then later David experiences Absalom's attempted overthrow and has to flee Jerusalem. David's house imploded because the holiness that kept the family together had been despised.

Despised means to devalue or to think little of, even to the point of mocking. God saw that David was devaluing holiness and did not honor the covenant, so he lost the ground he had gained.

If you are leading a household, please understand there is great blessing when you live in agreement with God's covenant boundaries—but also know that God is not mocked, for whatsoever a person sows, that shall he also reap. I have heard it said that what a generation does in moderation, the next generation will do in excess.

In John 15:1-2, Jesus describes our position in Him by using the analogy of the vine and branches. *"I am the true vine, and My Father is the vinedresser [caretaker]. Every branch in Me that does not bear fruit, He takes away; and every branch that bears fruit, He prunes it so it may bear more fruit."*

Three quick points I should make from this parabolic story.

- First, the branches that don't bear won't be allowed to continue to hang on the vine.

- Second, Jesus says in verse 4 that it is absolutely imperative (my emphasis) to abide in the vine. The word abide literally means to pitch your tent as in nail down the pegs and live there.

- Third, there is a promise while living in intimacy with Jesus the vine—you can ask what you will and it will be done for you.

Some of us get disappointed and confused because we have tried the asking part but have not solidified the abiding part. Abiding is like holy boundaries; it is for exclusive rights to us. He doesn't want to share us with the world systems. Some are asking from a position of a broken off branch thinking they are tied to the true vine. We may be hitched to some vine but not necessarily to the true and only vine that the Father oversees as a covenant vine. In His vineyard there is fruitfulness without the worry of any outside interference. Bring your home into the vineyard of the Lord and see the prosperity grow.

Second Corinthians 10:14-15 says that we will not boast beyond our measure, but within the measure of the sphere within God apportioned to us as a measure, to reach even as far as you. Apostle Paul is defending his boundary of influence. He correctly is identifying the extension of his ministry. He also says it is necessary to stay inside the sphere of influence that God had given him. Paul had stated that he might be an apostle to everyone, but he was to those who were in his sphere of grace. He wanted the Corinthians to know that he was not overextending his measure of influence because he was one of the first to bring them the Gospel. In verse 15 it is clear that what extends his influence is the measure in which others had grown in their faith.

Through covenant we are to have influence. That influence is based on the portion that God allows each of us to have. It must be recognized that it is the power of His covenant that has afforded us this influence. Not at any time should we start to think that through personal power or ability was the influence extended. The measure of influence is measured by the faith of those who are receiving from the measure that God has apportioned to the one carrying influence. The influence we have on our children should be seen as influence God has granted us. Therefore if that influence is traded for personal gain, we are despising the holiness of God by which we are to guard. When this sphere of influence is kept intact, it will grow faith in those we have been allowed to influence.

Again from John 15 Jesus says unless you stay connected to the vine there will not be any fruit. Some people after a season of fruitfulness will extend themselves beyond their influence that

God has given, and in the process become consumed with the new territory; they do not realize they had been disconnected from the life source of their ministry. It is wise on their part to recognize the overreach and return to the intimacy of Christ who is the extender of their sphere. Many have shipwrecked due to self-promotion and personal ambition. When the tent is firmly pitched and embedded in the truth, it is amazing the extension we can have when the promotion is coming from Him.

In 2000, Bruce Wilkinson wrote a book titled *The Prayer of Jabez*—it sold millions of copies and was number one on *The New York Times* bestsellers list. The prayer that Jabez prayed was fairly short, and he was not known for anything beyond the passage in First Chronicles 4:10 which reads: *"Oh that You would bless me indeed and enlarge my border, and that Your hand might be with me, and that You would keep me from harm that it may not pain me!"* And God granted what Jabez requested. The only other mention in the Bible about Jabez is that he was more honorable than his brothers. There are two things that God said about Jabez being an honorable man: one, he feared God and believed in all that God commanded; I believe that drew God's attention to him. The second thing is that Jabez had the courage to even ask for these things and believed that God would do them. This is not arrogance because Jabez knew it would be God and that it was for the purpose of extending God's purposes, not just personal influence for control's sake. Otherwise it would not have been honorable to ask for these things for temporal reasons.

When we ask for extending our borders, we must keep in mind God answers this request for those who have right hearts and are in covenant with the true vine Jesus mentioned. Let's look at the four things Jabez requested:

1. *Oh that You would bless me.* There are many different words describing blessing. In short, I believe Jabez was saying, God I am asking that I would not fall short of all You intend for me.

2. *Enlarge my border.* Allow me to be a steward who will have influence so others are helped through my obedience.

3. *That Your hand might be with me.* Great request in saying, I don't want to do this on my own without You being there to guide me.

4. *Keep me from harm.* This is a prayer of wisdom because Jabez is expecting some big things to take place in this partnership with God. He is asking, God, keep me from the snares that others would put before me, and keep me from me so that I don't go beyond where You have ordained me to go.

It is interesting to note the mother of Jabez named him "pain." His last request from God was to keep him from harm, that it may not pain him. Part of his prayer was that he would not finish the way he started. She named him Jabez because of her pain at birth. Now he is asking, don't let my destiny be tied to my beginning or past. This reflects where many of us struggle. We may feel limited or unworthy to even ask God for these things because of our past or present circumstance. I believe right now as you read this that you have not wanted to dream again so you won't be disappointed. Allow the Holy Spirit to give you the same honorable heart as Jabez to believe God and to see yourself extending into new areas of faith. Lord Jesus, I ask for those who are touched by this that you will lift the limitations of fear and past failure and give them faith to see blessing coming their way, amen!

SECURING YOUR WALLS

Nehemiah is well-known for having undertaken one of the most ambitious construction projects in the Bible. When Nehemiah's brother arrived with news of how the exiles, who had returned to Jerusalem, were in great trouble and disgrace due to the lack of fortification, he wept (see Neh. 1:1-4). Nehemiah thought that without walls around Jerusalem, Israel would never be restored to rebuild the temple for worship. Without worship they would be defenseless against their enemies. Rebuilding the walls was critical in order for the nation of Israel to establish safety and reclaim what had been given them through covenant. In the final result, Nehemiah was successful in his plan and leadership of the wall project. The walls of Jerusalem that had laid in ruins for nearly a century and a half were rebuilt in a record fifty-three days due to the willingness of the people and his influence to keep them focused on the task. Nehemiah was constantly confronting their enemies who were filled with threats and inflicting fear on the people. The mockery was relentless at times serving only to slow the work. Once the last breach in the wall was sealed, the harassment stopped and those who were not Jews who had been controlling the storehouse were thrown out.

Now that peace and safety had been restored, there was a new sense of hope starting to bloom. This made way so that later on the temple was rebuilt and worship once again brought the blessing of God. Nehemiah knew that securing the boundaries of Jerusalem was essential for God's Kingdom to grow. Likewise, as we learn to extend our boundaries through covenant, it is important that we learn to secure and strengthen them. We may gain new areas of responsibility or personal wealth, but unless the new boundaries are secured, we may not be able to hold them.

Nehemiah was taken into Babylon and served as the "cup-bearer" for the king. He was loyal, and could be trusted with the life of the king. His job was to taste the wine ahead of the king to ensure the wine was free from poison. Nehemiah had a good job by the standards of the day, especially for a slave. Two things of importance I should point out here. The first is God chose one who did not have to get involved because he was not living in Jerusalem. God gave him the passion for the job. Second, Nehemiah went from being a wine taster to one of the most influential people at the right time for God's plan of restoration.

God takes people who are virtually unknown and brings them to the forefront of need in just a flash if they are willing. Nehemiah was willing to leave the comfort of the king's palace to a place with no infrastructure. He accepted the challenge because he knew God was with him. You may be in preparation and being repositioned for such an extension for the Kingdom of God. Just like David was unknown until he found his cause—a loud-mouthed giant mocking the armies of God. God has a way of uncovering our hidden-ness to bring us to our moment of influence. Are you ready if He called upon you to make leaps of faith to extend your border so that others' faith may grow? You are a cupbearer today being prepared for Kingdom building tomorrow.

> *Father God, the Lord of our Covenant,*
>
> *We ask that the border of our lives be secure through Your holiness. May our families live the peace that comes through Your covenant! Help us to see ourselves the way You see us. Remove the fear of failure so we are ready to extend the pegs of our tent. Fill us with the passion*

we need to pursue every opportunity You bring our way. Give us the eyes of the Spirit to recognize Your hand upon us for good. Set us into our place to be watchmen on the wall to declare on earth what You are saying. Give us this day the knowledge of Your plans.

Amen!

11

PROSPERITY THROUGH COVENANT

Therefore if anyone is in Christ, he is a new creature
[species]; the old things passed away; behold,
new things have come (2 CORINTHIANS 5:17).

———◆———

I N THIS LAST chapter I want to end with application of the changes that may be ahead for some who will choose to embrace covenant in a deeper level. When these changes are made they will strengthen relationships and especially your marriage. They will help you also expect prosperity in every part of life. Prosperity at any level is not an accident, it is a principle of covenant. In part by how we view prosperity as something we are given to enlarge the Kingdom of God and not just for our own comfort level.

Prosperity simply means fullness. It could be fullness in peace, or in body, or financial increase. At any level we are to be rich in Christ our Covenant Redeemer. Paul's reference to being a new creation was in reference to someone entering into the New

Covenant. The New Covenant is not an old covenant with only a few improvements, it is completely different. Jesus said that He had fulfilled the Old Covenant. There is nothing more needed because it was used to bring us to the point of intimacy with Him.

With a New Covenant comes a new heart, one that is tender toward Him to the point He can write a new program upon it. We will learn a language of blessing and be set free from the old tongue of cursing. The Old Covenant was about the "doing" that satisfied it. The New is about "being," learning to be sons and daughters and not slaves. Jesus said in John 15:15, *"No longer do I call you slaves, for the slave does not know what his master is doing; but I have called you friends, for all things that I have heard from My Father I have made known to you."* So one of the changes in embracing covenant is enjoying the new position—from working for Him to working with Him. The difference now as a friend, we enter the house in a place of covenant not a place of labor, and we get to hear what is going to happen. Slaves had no prophetic insight.

As new creations in Christ we now hear from Him, not just about Him. Notice the reference of Christ being in us, not just with us. Now that He is in us, we carry covenant inside all the time and we speak from a position of covenant. Greater is He who is in us than he that is in the world. The Bible also tells us that if anyone is to speak let him or her speak as an oracle or mouthpiece of God. The changes that we need to apply by understanding covenant are to be more conscious of the Covenant Keeper who is resident inside us—and everything changes from that point.

According to Revelation 19:10, the spirit of prophecy is the testimony of Jesus. Wow! Now we are really embracing covenant because some think that prophecy doesn't even exist today. Jesus didn't wipe out the New Testament to fit our beliefs. He really is in us wanting to speak words of life to others through us. My point here is for us to realize that we are more than a bag of bones just waiting for the end of time—instead we are carrying the Ark of the Covenant, the glory of God inside us. We are to be a place of mercy just like the Mercy Seat that was on top of the Ark of the Covenant. Inside of us is the word of God just like the pot of manna was in the old. We carry the authority of Christ just like Aaron's rod that was placed in the Ark. We were gnarly humanity like the hard-to-work-with acacia wood. Then the pure gold covered the box and it had changed from a common piece of handmade furniture to a one-of-a-kind box that held the glory of God. You and I are uniquely and wonderfully made; yes, we are one of a kind and we carry His DNA. When the blood was placed on the Mercy Seat, it was deemed holy. When we received Christ and His forgiveness, His blood over us redeemed us to be holy, and holiness marks the boundaries of our lives making us in covenant with Him. Let the Glory come!

MORE BOATS PLEASE

Jesus was drawing a crowd by the lake of Gennesaret; there were two boats at the water's edge. The fishermen were out of their boats washing their nets (see Luke 5:2). Jesus got into one of the boats that just happened to be Simon Peter's. It should be obvious, but I don't want to just assume you will catch this point. Jesus, led of the Spirit, knows where your boat is and will get in if you are ready to cooperate with His plan. He asks Simon to push out a bit from the edge of the water so He could speak to the crowd. Notice the progression here. Jesus, representing the covenant, starts out by asking to be pushed just a little way out from shore. Then after He finished speaking, He told Peter to launch out into the deep water and let down his nets for a catch (see Luke 5:4). The first time He asked Peter, the second time He said to Peter. The more we allow the covenant to take control of the boat, the more we have to trust that He is up to something bigger than our understanding.

Peter at first begins to explain the natural laws of fishing, being the experienced fisherman that he was. Perhaps Peter was thinking, *We have tried all night and caught nothing, but it might be easier just to go along with Him to show Him the fish are not moving in our direction right now.* When Peter acquiesced and let down the nets, he soon realized there were so many fish that his nets were too weak to hold them all. Peter had to signal for his partner to come with another boat; and after they filled both boats, they began to sink. This revelation brought about a change in Peter to the point that he left his fishing business and followed Jesus. The turning point for Peter was when he agreed to go deeper.

The word deeper here *(bathos)* means mystery or beyond what you can sense. The change that comes when you agree to go deeper with Christ is remarkable. Peter caught so many fish that day that as a commercial fisherman he could have lived off that catch for a good while. Going deeper sometimes means going beyond what you actually see with your natural senses at the time; the end result is not just your boat being full, it includes the effects on those around you.

One of the principles of prosperity is that God will take what we have and use it for multiplication. It was Peter's boat to do with what he chose. He could have chosen to not oblige Jesus his boat as a stage to speak from; he could have chosen not to take the next step of going deeper and ultimately to following Jesus all the way to death and resurrection. Some of us are waiting for God to send a big check in the mail when there may be something you already possess that He will ask for to multiply. For instance, when God was calling Moses to return to Egypt and to show him that He would go with him, God asked, "What is that in your hand?" Moses answered, "A staff," a rod or stick (see Exod. 4:2). God told Moses to throw his rod down; and when Moses threw his rod on the ground, it became a snake and Moses ran from it. God spoke to him again to catch the snake by the tail, and when he did, it became a rod again (see Exod. 4:3-4).

Exodus 4:20 says that Moses returned to Egypt and he also took the staff of God. It started out as Moses' rod but when he gave it to God, it became something else. When he returned to Egypt it was now the Rod of God. Something common became holy when given over into the hands of God. Things multiply when we allow God to take ownership. Because of covenant He gives it back multiplied, more than when it was only in our possession. Jesus fed more than 5,000 people when a little boy handed over his lunch for one. In covenant, things are multiplied and they become supernatural.

David declared in Psalm 23:5, Lord, *"You prepare a table before me in the presence of my enemies; You have anointed my head with oil; my cup overflows."* All of these would be considered small except he said, God, You did this. God doesn't do things on a micro scale. First off, only God could place David in the middle of enemies and and enable him to eat with supernatural peace. Nothing annoys the devil more than to eat in front of him while he is threatening you. Second, it is the Lord who anoints his head, so that means he is being set apart for something huge to come. Last, God overflows his cup. In our Western mind, a cup would be small container, one that you would use to drink coffee or tea. A cup in David's time would be similar to a watering trough that all the animals could come and drink from. David's revelation of God was that He does big things when small things are yielded to Him.

Mary was consumed with being with Jesus and listening to him teach. Martha her sister comes to Jesus complaining:

> *"Lord, do You not care that my sister has left me to do all the serving alone? Then tell her to help me." But*

the Lord answered and said to her, "Martha, Martha, you are worried and bothered about so many things; but only one thing is necessary, for Mary has chosen the good part, which shall not be taken away from her" (Luke 10:40-42).

The deeper we enter into covenant, the more things we find are less important. Look for those things that really make a difference and give them priority, and you will see prosperity in things that appear to be common; but when He is present, drop all other less important issues and make Him the center of your attention, and you will find the other issues have been taken care of with less frustration.

WHAT DO YOU HAVE IN YOUR HOUSE?

One of the secrets of prosperity is that you are worth more than you think you are. Poverty is a spirit and it is not about the lack of money. Poverty is the fear of losing what you have. There are wealthy people who have a poverty spirit working against them. Some of them live in fear they will have a lawsuit hit them or some tragedy will take all they have acquired. Job said that which he feared had come upon him. Job was continually offering sacrifice in case one his children did something that would bring a curse. The fear became an attraction for the kingdom of darkness. Fear brings things about that are dark, just like faith brings about good in the Kingdom of God.

Second Kings 4:1-2 says that one of the prophets died and left his wife with two sons who were going to be sold to the creditors because of their debt. Elisha asked the wife, "What do you have in the house?" She said she had nothing in the house except a jar of oil. Notice that to her it seemed like she had nothing—until God multiplied it. Elisha told her to go and borrow as many vessels as she could. She was to pour her jar of oil into the empty vessels. To the natural mind covered in poverty, this won't make any sense. She obeyed the prophet and she continued to fill vessels until there was not one more vessel left (see 2 Kings 4:3-7).

The principle is that if you try to hide what you have and not make it available for God to touch it, then it will always be just a jar of oil. What seemed insignificant to one becomes significant to God. Another principle is that the oil flow was equal to the capacity of the empty pots. Empty is an opportunity for fullness. The oil stopped when there was no more capacity for the oil to flow. She sold the oil and paid her debt.

YOUR OFFERING BECOMES YOUR WEAPON

Judges 6:11-18 is the account when Israel was hiding from the Midianites. The sons of Israel were hiding in caves and were in constant fear of raids. After they had sown their seeds and were ready to harvest their crops, Midian along with other nations would come and pillage and steal everything from Israel. They cried out to God for help and God moved upon the most unassuming one of them all—Gideon. When the angel comes to him he is hiding, hoping to save some of the wheat for bread. The angel called him a valiant warrior, which in the natural was the farthest thing from reality. God saw in Gideon that his weakness could become God's strength. Gideon asked the angel, "If the Lord is with us, then where are the miracles that are fathers told us about?" (see Judg. 6:13). Gideon didn't realize he was getting ready to be one of those historical markers. Gideon wanted a little more proof that what he was seeing was true. He told the angel, "If you are for real, then wait here and I will go and prepare an offering and return." The angel agreed. In spite of the scarcity of food, Gideon brought a goat and some bread. The angel touched the offering and it was consumed in the fire.

In Judges 7, Gideon is getting somewhat bolder. He decides to go spy on the Midianites. He overhears one of the Midian soldiers reciting a dream he had. The dream, in short, was a large loaf of bread that rolled into their camp and destroyed their tents. His pagan friend interprets his dream, which I find hilarious; one pagan dreaming and another giving the interpretation. Anyway, here it is, *"This is nothing less than the sword of Gideon the son of Joash, a man of Israel; God has given Midian and all the camp into his hand."* The very offering that Gideon offered, God used his offering as a weapon. The power of an offering can bring about the most unusual results. Gideon had the courage, he now needed to deliver Israel from the terror of their enemy.

THANKFULNESS—KEY TO PRESERVING PROSPERITY

First Thessalonians 5:18 says that in everything we are to give thanks, for this is the will for you in Christ Jesus. I'm sure you would agree it is simply good manners to be thankful. Most define thankfulness as being appreciative. If someone does something nice for you, you would reply with a thank you. Thankfulness in this context of Scripture has a different meaning than a casual response. The word has two parts EU, which means to express, and a derivative of Christ. The two together is the word Eucharist, which means the Body of Christ. Some groups call the Lord's Table or Communion, the Eucharist. If we place Eucharist into the verse it would read, In everything be or give the Body of Christ. Being thankful is expressing the Body of Christ and taking the opportunity to express what Jesus would say and do while here on earth. Paul further says being the Eucharist is the will (inheritance) in Christ Jesus. Anytime you bless someone or stop to pray for someone, you are being thankful or full of the Eucharist, the Body of Christ.

Psalm 100:4 says, *"Enter His gates with thanksgiving and His courts with praise. Give thanks to Him, bless His name."* One translation says when you enter His gates the password is *thanksgiving.* The importance of the gates leads me to my point on prosperity. In biblical history the gates were symbolic for a number of things. The elders of the city would sit at the gate and act as judges over matters. They would screen visitors as they approached the gate for security purposes. Commerce was conducted around the gates. People bought and sold their goods there. The next level was to enter into the city, which were the courts. If you were going to gain access to the king, you first had to enter the courts. Notice the progression and who could enter the gates must be part of the Body of Christ, the Eucharist—it could be said that we must be in His covenant to go deeper into the city. The courts were all about praise; the attention and focus is all about His goodness and His love toward us. Prosperity took place not outside the gates but inside. Covenant is not about standing around the edges, it is about being baptized into the Body of Christ. Expressing His attributes is the password to enter those gates to prosper, and real prosperity is inside His gates.

When you see the term Bride of Christ, it is referring to our position in Heaven; the term Body of Christ is our activity here on earth. We will be the Bride of Christ and enjoy the Marriage Supper of the Lamb, but right now we are functioning as His arms and feet and extending His will on earth. Colossians 1:27 tells us that the mystery among the Gentiles has now been revealed which is Christ in us the hope of glory.

Philippians 4:6 says, *"Be anxious for nothing, but in everything by prayer and supplication with thanksgiving, let your requests be made known to God."* Supplication is a very specific and targeted request. This specific request is made with thanksgiving. The best way to understand this type of prayer is to see yourself as the Eucharist or Body of Christ praying. If Jesus were praying that prayer on earth, it would be viewed as if He was interceding for the request. Praying with thanksgiving is more than using the term thanks, it is being one who the Holy Spirit would pray through as He did through Jesus. Jesus said to us in John 16:15 that the Holy Ghost would come and dwell in us and He would take the things that belong to Christ and reveal them to us. The Holy Spirit really wants to show us how we can be the Body of Christ in the earth expressing the same things that Jesus did when He walked here.

Jesus in prayer said to God, *"The words which You gave Me I have given to them"* (John 17:8). Jesus gave the people words and teachings that caused them to believe that Jesus was the one sent by the Father to bring the New Covenant. Inside of the New Covenant we are given words of life. I am not just referencing vocabulary type words but more like specific supplication words that are given for the purpose of targeting the issue at hand.

WORDS THAT PREVAIL

I believe this is how Jesus gives us words that cause us to prevail in supplication: *"In the same way the Spirit also helps our weakness [inability]; for we do not know how to pray as we should, but the Spirit Himself intercedes for us with groanings [unknown language] too deep for words"* (Rom. 8:26). Verse 27 furthers this truth by saying, *"He who searches the hearts knows what the mind of the Spirit is, because He intercedes for the saints according to the will of God."* Remember, Jesus told us that when He left He would send the Holy Spirit, the Spirit of Truth, and He would guide us into all (not partial or half) truth. Jesus knew His followers would need help in prayer and understanding all that He had said. Sending the Holy Spirit was part of the promise given to those who received His covenant.

Acts 1:4-5 says, *"Gathering them together, He commanded them not to leave Jerusalem, but to wait for what the Father had promised, 'Which,' He said, 'you heard of from Me; for John baptized with water, but you will be baptized with the Holy Spirit not many days from now.'"* Just a reminder here that a promise is received inside the covenant. Being in covenant gives you the right to receive promises. Jesus was commanding them not to do anything until they received the promise of the Father, which was the baptism of the Holy Spirit.

Since there are times when I really don't know the prevailing words to pray, I have the promise of my Father that tells me to let the Holy Spirit in me take over, He is part of the covenant promise that will bring me to the full intentions that God has for me—and you. In First Corinthians 14:2, Paul is instructing the church in Corinth that the *"one who speaks in a* [unknown] *tongue does not speak to men but to God; for no one understands, but in his spirit he speaks mysteries."* Wow, that is amazing when you consider the power that is in the promise of the Father. I can be praying about things that my conscious mind doesn't comprehend. The word mystery *(bathos)* is the same word Jesus used to tell Peter to launch out into the deep, mystery. It actually means to go where your natural senses are not directing. When the Holy Spirit prays through you, Paul is saying you are praying for others to hear you or even to understand you; but when you are interceding for deep things, your mind would simply get in the way or think this is too good to be true. Doubt and unbelief can't enter into the supplication. I pray that you will receive the promise that He has for you.

One last promise that excites me when I think of how God is so redemptive in all He does. In Genesis 3, the reference is after the Fall of Adam, verse 24 says, *"So He drove man out; and at the east of the garden of Eden He stationed the cherubim, and the flaming sword which turned every direction to guard the way to the tree of life."* Most of my life I have been taught that the cherubim were there to keep man out of the Garden and perhaps after the Fall that was true; but God says that He will make all things new (see Acts 3:19). Jesus, the Second Adam, who redeemed us, wants us to now eat from the Tree of Life. The reference was to guard the way to the Tree of Life; the word guard means to keep the way. In my mind I see the Angel with the flaming sword lighting the way like a landing strip for a jumbo jet, saying, "This is the way, come on in and enjoy My habitation for you."

Lord Jesus,

Thank You for opening a new and living way for us. I pray that none reading this book will come short of the glory You have wanted to give all who live in Your covenant. I pray that the power of the Holy Spirit would be received so we might know Your fullness. I pray that the covenant You have made available to all of us would not just be a teaching but would be our life. Thank You, Father, for sending Your Son, our Redeemer.

Amen!

ABOUT THE AUTHOR

For more information on Kerry Kirkwood's ministry, go to www.trinityfellowship.com